MAKING MODEL CARS

For thousands of years, road travellers
were restricted to the speed of their legs –
or if they were lucky, that of their horses.
Consequently, few people travelled more
than twenty miles from their home!

With the invention of the petrol engine
and development of motor cars, more and
more people were able to own their own
car and travel quickly to work or to
friends, over long distances. Our whole
world has changed.

MAKING MODEL CARS includes early
vintage models, high-powered,
streamlined modern vehicles, and, in these
days of growing petrol shortage, smaller
fuel-saving cars too – all with detailed
plans and easy to follow instructions.

MAKING MODEL CARS
A CAROUSEL BOOK 0 552 54154 0

First published in Great Britain in 1979

PRINTING HISTORY
Carousel edition published 1979

Text and illustrations copyright © Peter Fairhurst 1979

Carousel Books are published by
Transworld Publishers Ltd.,
Century House,
61–63 Uxbridge Road,
Ealing, London W5 5SA.

Filmset by Keyspools Ltd, Golborne, Lancs.
Made and printed by The Guernsey Press Co. Ltd., Guernsey,
Channel Islands.

MAKING MODEL CARS

Written and illustrated by
Peter Fairhurst

CAROUSEL BOOKS
A DIVISION OF TRANSWORLD PUBLISHERS LTD.

Other books by PETER FAIRHURST

MAKING MODEL AEROPLANES
MAKING MODEL TRANSPORT VEHICLES
MAKING A MODEL VILLAGE

All published by Carousel Books

Introduction

This book contains plans and instructions for building models of cars mainly from card and balsa wood.

The subjects range from 1913 to the present time and all the models are made to the same scale: they are 1/32nd of full size. Each metre of the original vehicle is represented by 3 cm on the model (1 foot becomes $\frac{3}{8}$ in).

This scale is used in many plastic construction kits, slot-car racing models and the vehicles in *Making Model Transport Vehicles* (published by Carousel Books) so you can make the cars in this book and use or display them with other models built to the same scale.

The models are arranged in order of difficulty. The first section is modern cars, beginning with the Volkswagen Golf, the construction of which is described in detail. The same instructions cover the cars which follow. The different technique required for the later cars in the first section is described for the Ferrari and covers the rest of the first section.

The second section is made up of four vintage cars. Construction of the Mercedes is described in detail and the instructions should be referred to when building the other vehicles.

Each model has a brief history, a list of parts required to make it, instructions and plans for each of the parts.

Contents

The models are arranged in the following order:–

SECTION 1   **Modern Vehicles**   **Page**

Volkswagen Golf	18
Renault 5	25
Microdot	32
Lagonda	39
Citroen 2 CV 6	47
Fiat X1–9	55
Ferrari Boxer	63
Pontiac Firebird Trans Am.	71
Lotus Esprit	80

SECTION 2   **Vintage Cars**

Targa Florio Mercedes	87
Bugatti Type 59	97
Ford Model T	104
Rolls Royce Phantom II	114

Making the models

The models in this book are divided into two types. The majority of them are modern cars and the models are built, like the full size vehicles, with a complete body shell to which the wheels, bumpers, etc., are added to complete the model. The models of the older cars have to be built, as the originals were, on a base or chassis to which the bodywork, axles, wheels etc., are added.

The modern car models are generally less complicated and easier to make so these are dealt with in the first part of the book, the Vintage cars make up the second section.

All the models are made to the same scale and are 1/32nd of full size. Each metre of the full size car is represented by 3 cm on the model (1 foot to $\frac{3}{8}$ in).

The following pages describe, in detail, the building of the **Volkswagen Golf**. Read through the instructions and look at the plans on page 22 so that you understand the construction method before you begin. If you then follow the instructions carefully, stage by stage, you should have no difficulty in making the first model. These same instructions apply to each of the models in the first section, so these models are built in the same way. Detail changes, however, are described when necessary.

There is one important thing to remember. The care you take in making a model will be reflected in the finished work. If you rush the work and take short cuts the model will not be as good as it would have been if you had taken more time and worked carefully.

Before you start you will need:

TOOLS

Sharp pencil/ball-point pen
Ruler
Compass
Scissors (medical scissors are excellent)
Craft knife

MATERIALS

Thin card
Carbon paper
Glue – white P.V.A. is probably the
    best
Balsa wood
Paint – Acrylic/Polymer colours or
    emulsion
Varnish – Polymer varnish or 'Cold
    Glaze'
(available from model or hobby shops)

GENERAL INSTRUCTIONS

1. Place a piece of card under the plan of the base of the model.

2. Hold the book firmly and prick the end of each straight line with the point of your compass.

3. Remove the card from the book. You will have a series of compass pricks. These points must now be joined up, using a pencil and ruler and taking care that you join the right dots – check that your finished drawing is the same as the original.

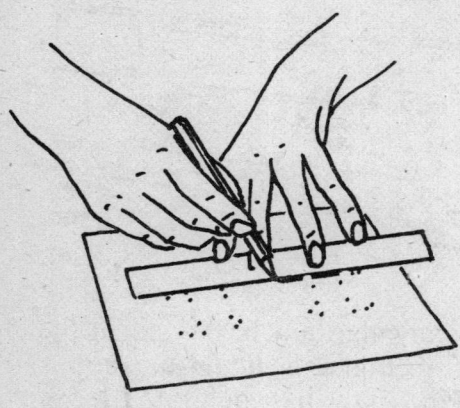

4. Using ruler and compass, score all the broken lines.

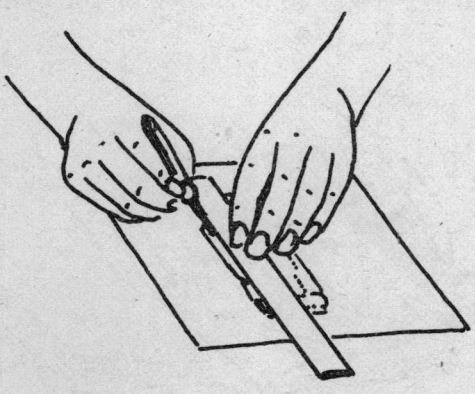

Cut out the base and fold the tabs to right angles

5. The large tabs at the four wheel positions have to be made rigid to hold the wheels upright so they have to be strengthened as shown with small pieces of card.

Wheel supports

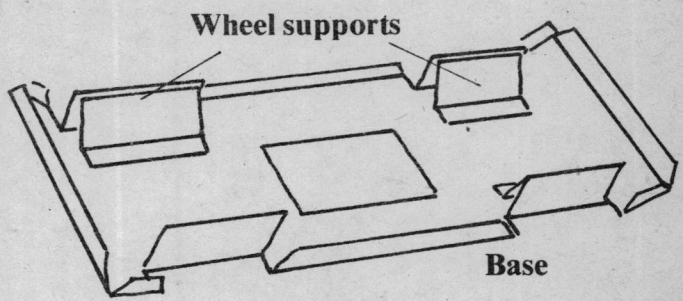

Base

The rectangular hole in the base is to help in fitting the roof section and should be cut out at this stage. The arrow on the base points to the front of the car.

6. The two sides of the car have to be cut out next. The procedure is similar to that for the base but a sheet of carbon paper should be placed on top of the card.

7. Mark out the ends of each straight line as before and then draw in all curved lines with a pencil. You should also mark in all the body details, windows, etc.

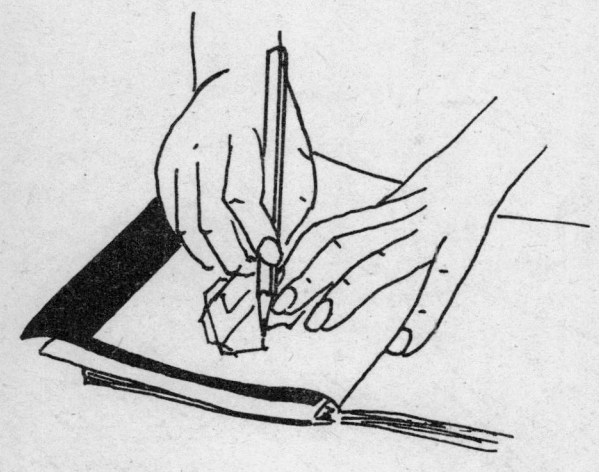

Remove the card, join the dots as before and redraw the carbon lines if necessary. Score and cut out. The second side is made from the same drawing but the windows and body details have to be put on the **wrong side** and the tabs folded the opposite way.

8. Cut out the two body bulkheads and then assemble the model as shown. Start by fixing the centre section of the sides to the base. Now glue in the bulkheads, the back one fits just in front of the rear wheel openings and the front one fits at the point where the top of the windscreen joins the roof.

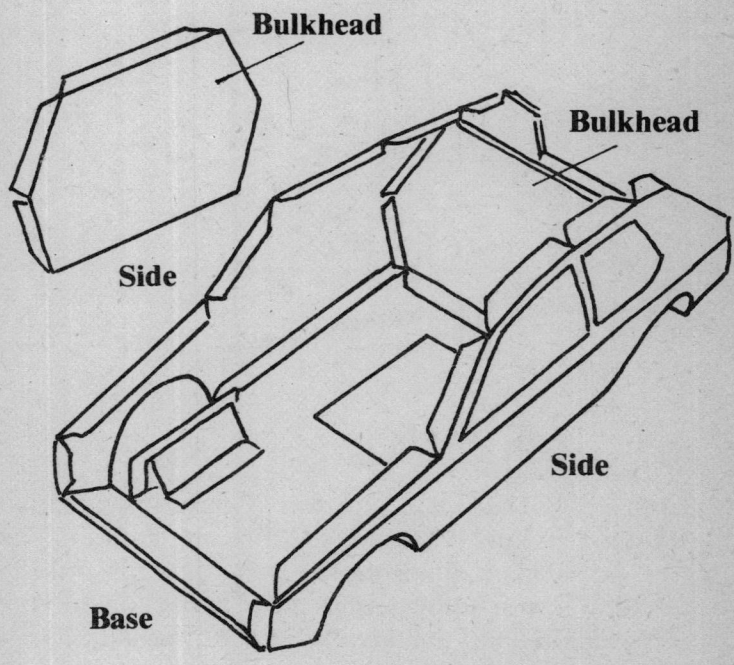

Bend up the front and rear sections of the base and glue the tabs – keep the model on a flat surface and make sure that it is not twisted.

9. Prepare the bonnet and the roof/windscreen sections, join the two together as shown to give the curve of the windscreen.

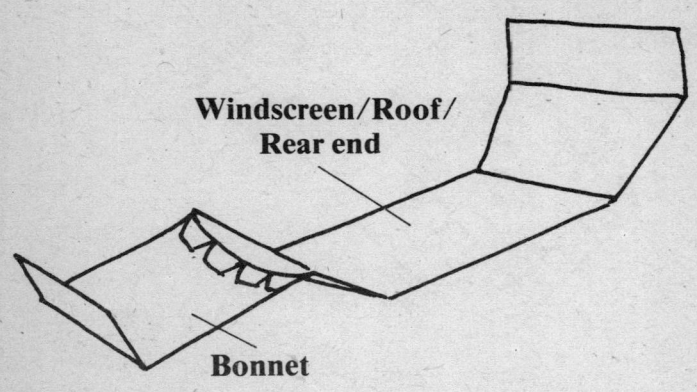

Windscreen/Roof/ Rear end

Bonnet

10. Starting with the bonnet and windscreen glue this piece in place, again being careful to keep the model square, then continue with the front end, the roof and finally the rear to complete the body.

Windscreen/Roof/Rear end

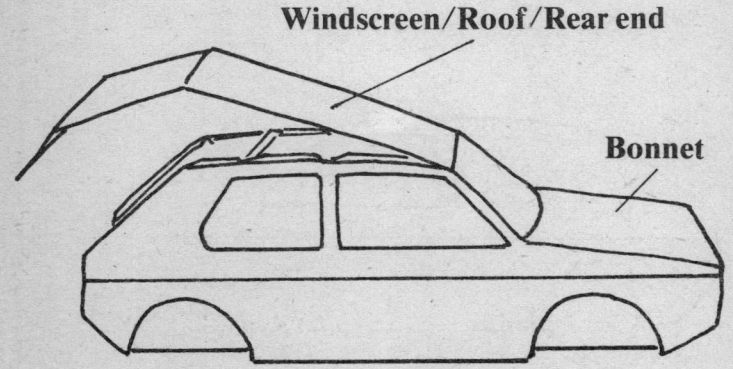

Bonnet

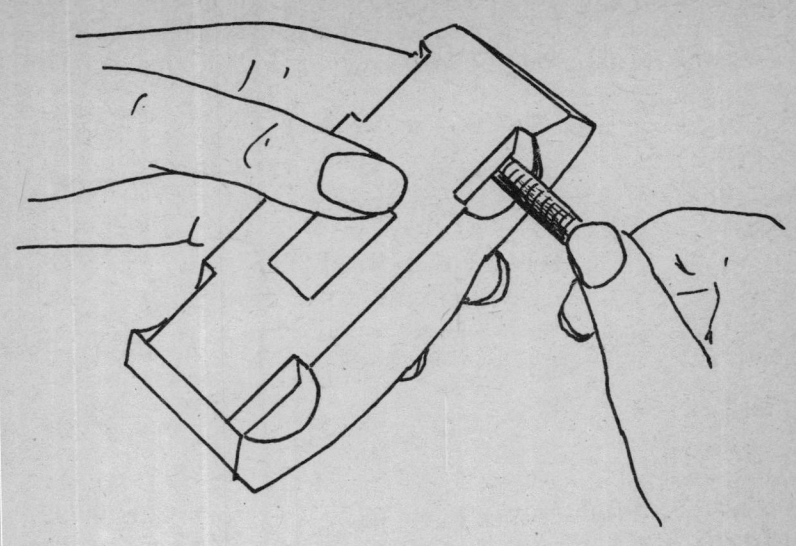

11. When the glue is quite dry you should **flare** the wheel openings. Use a round pencil to press the edge of the card to give the required effect.

12. Support the complete body on scraps of balsa wood while you glue the wheels in place.

FINISHING THE MODEL

Wheels

The most satisfactory way to make wheels for the models is from lengths of dowel of the right diameter. The dimensions are given for each model. Choose the correct size dowel and carefully saw off the wheels to the right size and then round off the edges with glasspaper. The wheel can then be painted matt black to represent the tyres, and the hubcaps can then either be painted on or made from a disc of coloured paper glued in place.

Bodywork

The body should be carefully painted (leaving the windows clear). When the paint is dry, mark in the body details with a black ball point pen and to make the windows more realistic, paint them with watered-down blue paint, dark at the top and lighter towards the bottom.

The finished model should then be varnished. You will probably need several coats to give a good shine. Be careful not to 'polish' the tyres and the bumpers if they are of the rubber type fitted to many modern cars.

Bumpers

Bumpers for many of the models are to be cut from strips or scraps of balsa wood. Where dimensions are given the bumpers are straight and of rectangular cross section. In other cases, shapes and cross sections are given.

Other details

Lights, number plates, etc., can be cut from suitable card and glued in place.

VOLKSWAGEN

At the turn of the Century Ferdinand Porsche was the technical director of the Austrian Austro-Daimler company and was a brilliant mechanical engineer. He was one of the true pioneers of the modern motor car and was always experimenting with new ideas. He developed a successful electric car to be used when petrol was in short supply during the First World War.

In 1916 Dr. Porsche was made Managing Director of Austro-Daimler, a post he held until 1923 when he moved to Stuttgart to work for the German Daimler Company where one of his first duties was to re-design the 1922 racing Mercedes which became the 1923 Targa Florio Mercedes and is one of the models in the second section of this book.

By 1929 Dr. Porsche was back in Austria and working for the Steyr Company where he developed a small 2-litre six cylinder car. His contract was terminated after only one year and Porsche had to decide what to do for the future. He considered his position; he had a great deal of experience and an excellent reputation so he moved back to Stuttgart and opened his own company to operate as consulting engineers, solve technical problems for manufacturers and design components and even complete cars for clients.

At this time, Porsche was designing a small rear engined car which he hoped would, one day, go into mass production. In 1934 the German government directed the company to design a 'people's car'. Porsche based the design for the new car on his own brainchild and the legendary Volkswagen 'Beetle' was born.

In 1938 a new factory to make the car was built at Wolfsburg but preparation for war meant that production of the car did not go ahead. Various military versions of the car were produced during the war and the first civilian vehicles were built towards the end of 1945. Production of the vehicle continued for about 30 years and 20 million cars were made, making the Beetle the best selling vehicle of all time, its nearest rival being the Model T Ford which sold about 15 million.

In the 1970's a new generation of Volkswagens was produced, the Golf, Passat and Polo. Our model is of the Golf, a small family saloon available with different sized four cylinder engines and either two or four doors. The body of the car was designed by the Italian stylist Giugiaro and is a typical car of the 70's having a **hatchback**, which is an opening rear section, to give access to the area behind the back seats in place of a more conventional boot.

VOLKSWAGEN   GERMANY

GOLF 3-door (2 plus hatchback)

Length: 3736 mm (146·5 ins)

Wheelbase: 2410 mm (94·5 ins)

Engine: 4 cylinders 1093 cc or 1470 cc
developing 50 b.h.p. or 70 b.h.p

The engine is mounted in the
front and drives the front wheels.

Parts required:

1 Base
4 Wheel supports
2 Sides
1 Bonnet
1 Windscreen/Roof/Rear end
4 Wheels 17 mm diameter × 5 mm
   (0·7 in × 0·2 in)
2 Bumpers. Balsa strip 3 mm × 2 mm
   ($\frac{1}{8}$ in × $\frac{1}{16}$ in)

Construction:

See general instructions on p. 10.

VOLKSWAGEN GOLF 3-door

VOLKSWAGEN GOLF 4-door

Plans

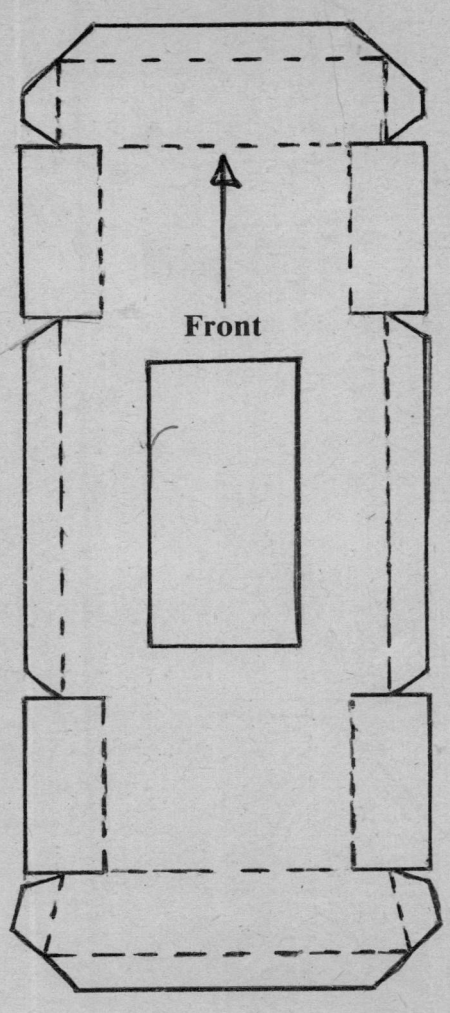

Front

Base

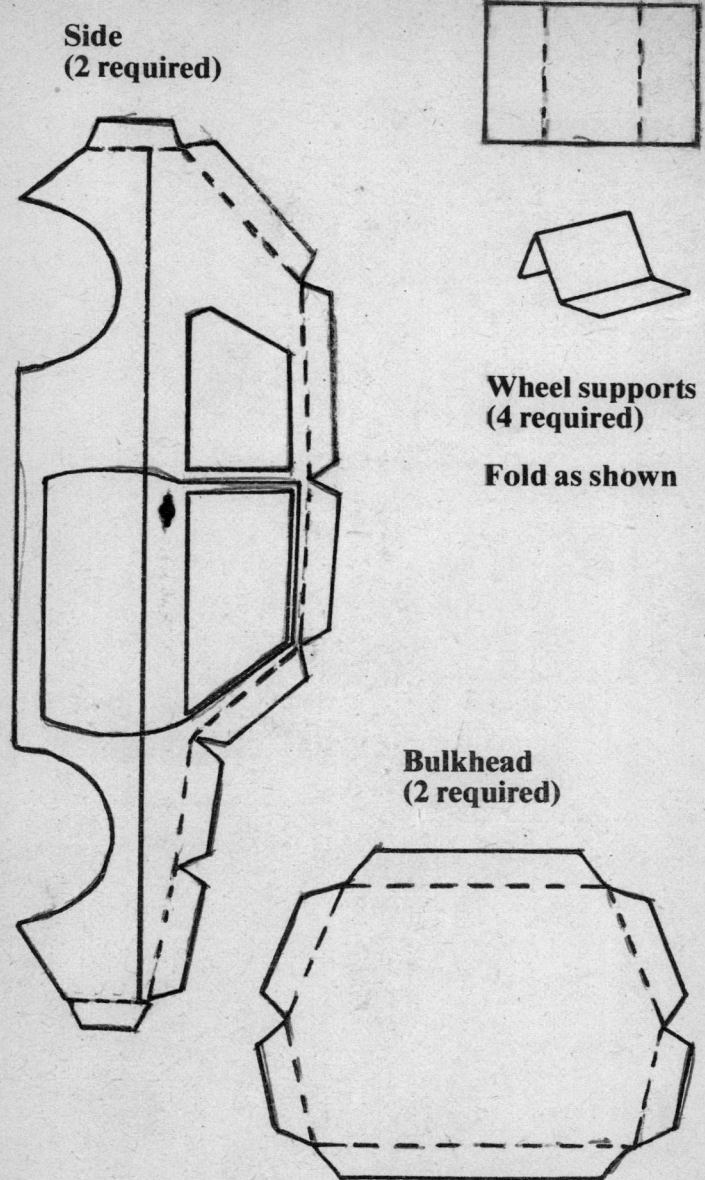

Side
(2 required)

Wheel supports
(4 required)

Fold as shown

Bulkhead
(2 required)

23

Windscreen/Roof/Rear end

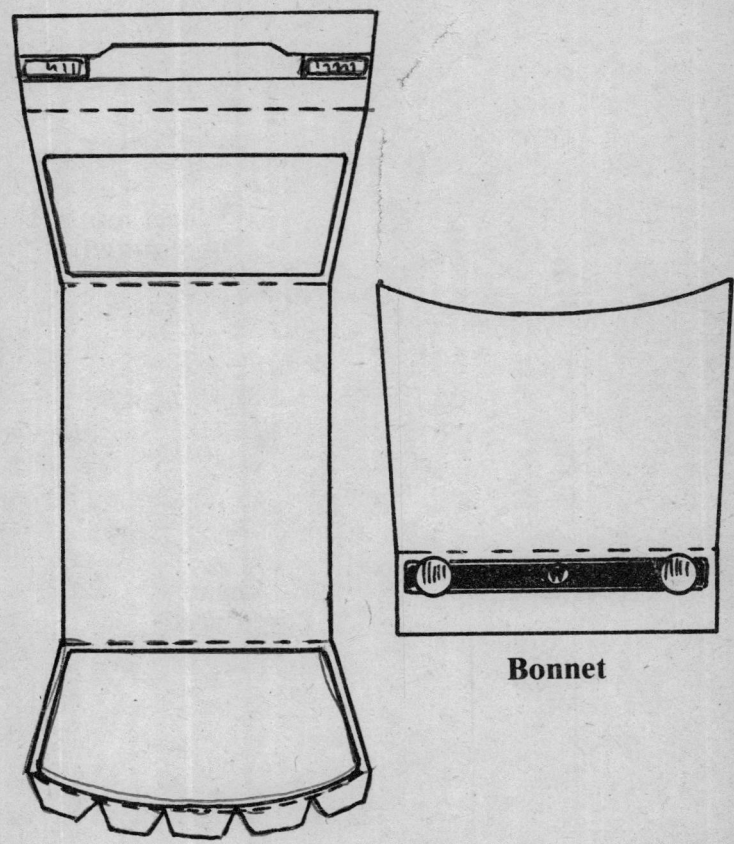

Bonnet

RENAULT

The story of Renault began in 1898 when Louis Renault built his first car in a small garden shed at Billancourt, near Paris. Louis was just 21 and his car was unusual for the time, having a three speed gearbox and rear axle as we know it today, instead of the almost universal chain drive.

The car was so good that friends wanted to own replicas and in 1899, Louis' brothers, Marcel and Fernand, joined him and the company Renault Freres was born.

To establish their name as motor manufacturers, the brothers entered cars, and were successful, in major races. In 1903 Marcel was killed while racing and that side of the business was stopped. In 1906, however, Renault were back in racing for the first ever Grand Prix. The race was held at Le Mans and Renault won it at a speed of 63.8 m.p.h. (102·72 km.p.h.). The car was fitted with the new Michelin invention of detachable wheel rims.

Fernand died in 1909 and Louis ran the business on his own and with considerable success. The majority of taxis in Paris, Berlin, London and New York were Renaults by the time the First World War temporarily put a stop to production, as the factory was taken over to help the war effort. In the years after the war, Renault production included lorries, buses, fire engines, tractors and marine and areo engines.

Car production continued to grow and record attempts were made to publicise the name. In 1925 a touring car averaged 100·39 m.p.h. (161·5 km.p.h.) for 12 hours at Montlhery and in 1926 a special bodied Renault became the first car to average more than 100 m.p.h. (160 km.p.h.) for 24 hours.

After the second World War, during which the company was taken over by the Germans, Renault became state owned but it was still run as a private, self-

RENAULT 5

supporting concern. In the immediate post-war years production was concentrated on small family saloons and several popular cars were made. Sporting activity has continued, in 1971 a Renault Alpine won the Le Mans 24 hour race and in 1973 the Alpine was 1st, 2nd, 3rd, 5th and 6th. The current production models range from very small cars to large luxurious family saloons and all have a front mounted engine driving the front wheels.

The model in this book is of the Renault 5, introduced in 1971 and awarded the title 'Best small car of the year'. Various engines are available making it an ideal small family car or a more sporting vehicle for those who buy the more powerful version.

RENAULT 5   FRANCE

Length: 3520 mm (138 ins)

Wheelbase: 2422 mm (95 ins)

Engine:	**5L**	**5TL**	**5TS**
	848 cc	956 cc	1289 cc
	36 b.h.p.	44 b.h.p.	64 b.h.p.

Parts required:

1 Base
4 Wheel supports (plan p. 23)
2 Sides
2 Bulkheads
1 Windscreen/Roof/Rear end
1 Bonnet
4 Wheels 17 mm diameter × 5 mm
  (0·7 in × 0·2 in)

Construction:

Construction of this model is quite straightforward. Follow the instructions for the first model and you should have no difficulty.

The bumpers on the actual car are moulded in polyester and appear as part of the shape of the car. On the model you should paint the front and rear sections grey to represent the originals.

Plans

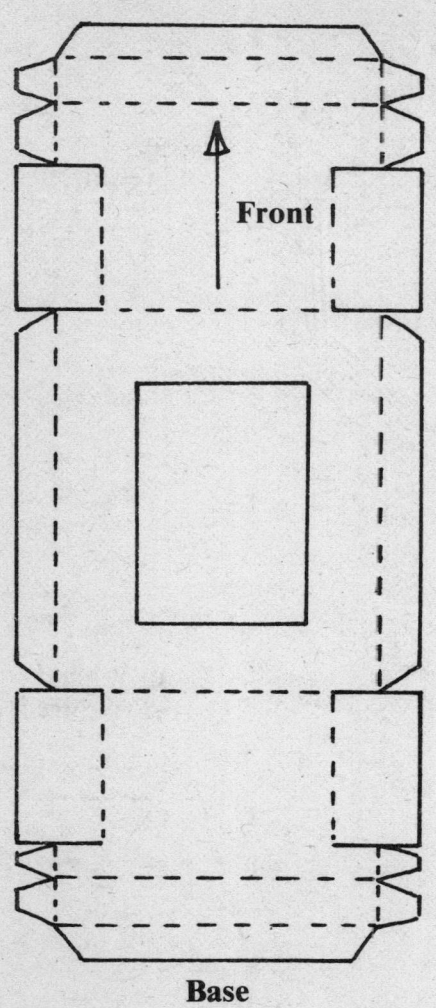

Front

Base

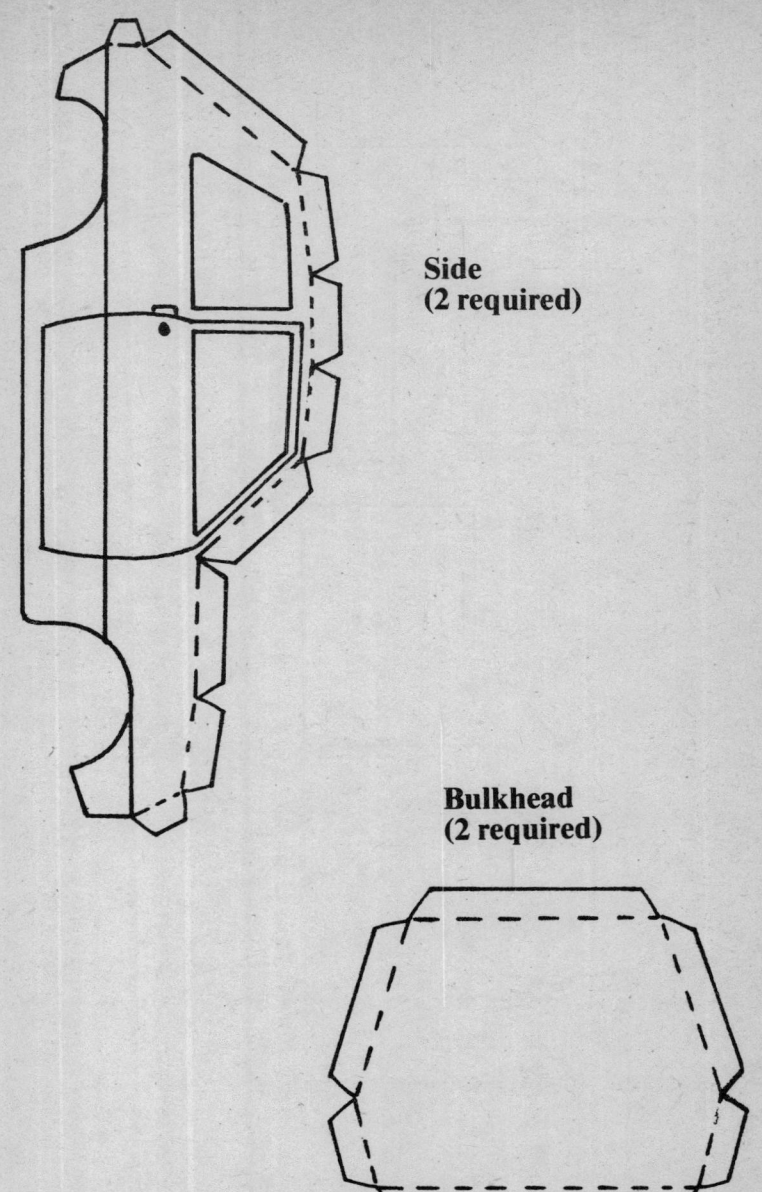

Side
(2 required)

Bulkhead
(2 required)

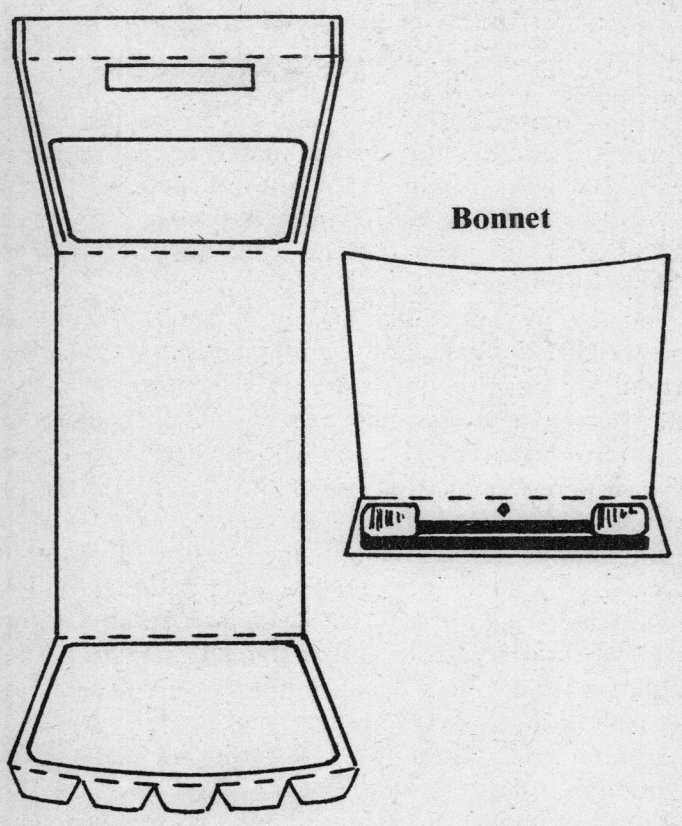

Bonnet

Windscreen/Roof/Rear end

MICRODOT

In the early days of the motor car the majority of vehicles had bodies designed and built by coachbuilders who had been building horse drawn carriages for many years. Designs were based on traditional carriage practice but over the years the 'horse-less carriage' gave way to the automobile as the craftsmen accepted the challenge of the 'new-fangled' machines.

With the rise in popularity of the motor car brought on by mass production and the manufacture of inexpensive vehicles, coach building became a specialised craft reserved for only the most expensive prestige cars which were often designed to suit the needs of the buyer and styled to suit his taste.

There has always been a place in the motor industry for the specialist designer and builder and in recent years, particularly since the last war, Italy has produced some great names. Among them are Pininfarina, Vignale, Ghia, Bertone, and many more who have produced exotic design studies exhibited at motor shows and body styling for mass produced vehicles.

Other countries also have their specialists. In England there are several including the freelance designer William Towns who styled the Rover BRM Gas Turbine Le mans car 1965. Towns also designed the DBS Aston Martin which, for many years, has been one of the most sought after cars in the world. The success of the DBS led Aston Martin to ask Towns to design the sensational new Lagonda.

William Towns has been working for some years on a most important aspect of motoring for the future. With roads becoming more congested and the need to conserve energy, a new type of car is required – a small economical vehicle – the city car. Towns' original city car was the Minissima which was based on B.M.C. Mini components

MICRODOT

and though the car was shorter than the Mini it was not the solution to the car problem.

The next model in the book is the Microdot. This is Towns' current city car project and may well become a production vehicle. It is very small and designed to carry three people, side by side. The car is electrically powered but, to overcome the excessive weight of batteries needed to give an electric car adequate performance and duration between charges, also has a powerful two-stroke engine driving a generator to keep the batteries charged.

Stored electrical power can be used around the town and generated power used on the open road and where more performance is required. This combination of electricity and petrol certainly seems to be the answer to the problem at the moment and will remain so until a new type of battery is found. Conventional batteries are large, heavy and expensive and store very little energy in comparison with a small tank of petrol.

MICRODOT   ENGLAND

Length: 1990 mm (78 ins)

Wheelbase: 1326 mm (52 ins)

Engine: Petrol/Electric

              A two-stroke engine drives a
              generator to supplement the
              power of the batteries.

Parts required:

1 Base
4 Wheel supports (plans p. 23)
2 Sides
1 Rear end
1 Windscreen/Roof
4 Wheels 16 mm diameter $\times$ 5 mm
$(\frac{5}{8}$ in $\times \frac{3}{16}$ in$)$

Construction:

This is a very small model and internal bulkheads are not needed. Prepare and assemble the base and sides as before.

Glue the rear end in place to the sides and the base, but do not stick the mudflaps, these should be folded to stick out slightly from the body.

The windscreen/roof section is fitted in the normal way.

The prototype Microdot was painted green and you will see from the drawings that the lower section of the sides and the rear are painted black.

The windows and the roof panel of the prototype are made from brown tinted glass.

Plans

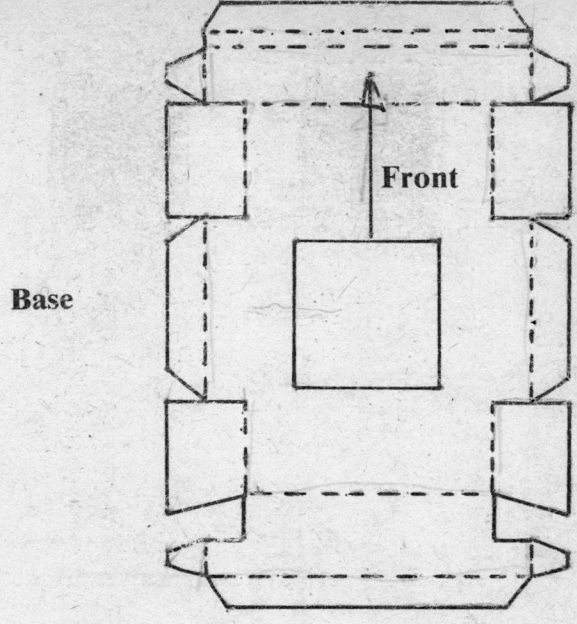

Base

Front

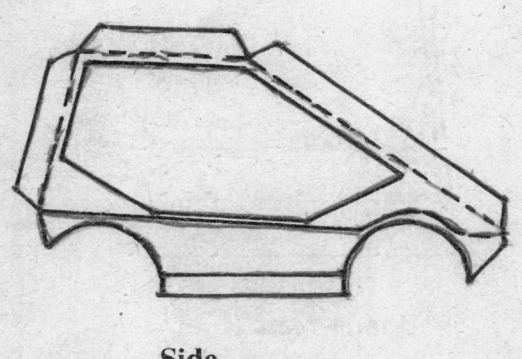

Side
(2 required)

37

Rear end

Windscreen/Roof

LAGONDA

An American opera singer and engineer named Wilbur Gunn came to England from his home-town of Lagonda Creek, Ohio, early in the century and around 1904 started a firm to build motor-cycles and light cars. He chose the name Lagonda for his firm and the vehicles produced. By 1913 the Lagonda was a good small four cylinder car with quite a good performance that was sold at a very low price and remained in production for many years. After World War One the engine size was increased and the car was, for several years, popular as a small high quality vehicle that was extremely economical. But, over the years, improvements and modifications made the car heavier and it's performance less lively, and during the 1920's most manufacturers were producing cars that cost much less than the Lagonda and offered a superior performance.

In 1925 the 2 litre Lagonda was announced. This new car was a very refined and smooth touring car with better than average performance and was produced for many years and with several different body styles.

During this time the Bentley was enjoying considerable success internationally and dominating the Le Mans 24 hour races but was financially unstable. Rolls Royce bought Bentley in 1931 and W. O. Bentley was employed by the owners. But, by 1935 he had left and gone to Lagonda where he was responsible for the design of some excellent cars which were fast, expensive and exclusive.

After the Second World War, Lagonda found themselves in financial difficulties and were bought out by the David Brown organisation and merged with Aston Martin. Financial difficulties developed again in the 1970's and Aston Martin Lagonda (1975) Limited was formed by a group of businessmen to continue building these famous cars.

At the 1976 London Motor Show, Aston Martin Lagonda caused a sensation with the revolutionary new Lagonda – a completely new concept of what a big luxury car could be. The mechanical side is based on the Aston Martin V8 giving the car outstanding performance. The body was designed by William Towns and is thoroughly modern in appearance. The interior of the car heralds a new era in electronic instrumentation and controls. There are no conventional instruments or switches (even the automatic transmission is controlled by touch buttons). Instrumentation is in the form of electronically-controlled graphic and digital displays replacing the usual dials and gauges.

The Lagonda is probably the most advanced production car in the world and combines the best traditions of the hand-built car with space-age technology.

LAGONDA   ENGLAND

Length: 5283 mm (17 ft 4 ins)

Wheelbase: 2915 mm (9 ft 6$\frac{3}{4}$ ins)

Engine: **V8** 5340 cc

                 Engine power details are
                 not quoted by the company.

LAGONDA

Parts required:

1 Base
4 Wheel supports (plan p. 23)
2 Sides
2 Bulkheads
1 Bonnet
1 Tapered bonnet
1 Windscreen/Roof/Window
1 Boot
4 Wheels 20 mm diameter × 6 mm
  (0·8 in × 0·25 in)
2 Bumpers – balsa wood 5 mm × 3 mm
  ($\frac{3}{16}$ in × $\frac{1}{8}$ in)

Construction:

Construction of the Lagonda is quite straightforward. The tapered bonnet and radiator piece is glued in place after the main bonnet is fitted.

The bumpers are made from strips of balsa wood glued in place, sanded and painted black.

Plans

Front

Base

43

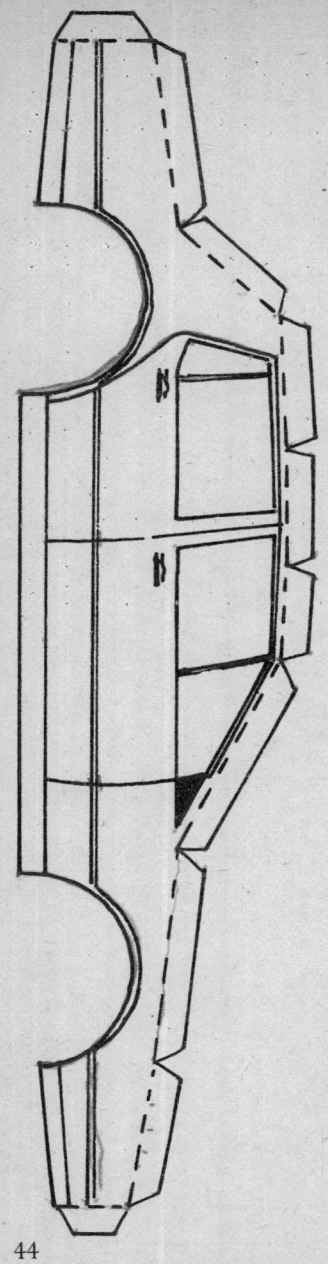

Side
(2 required)

Bulkhead
(2 required)

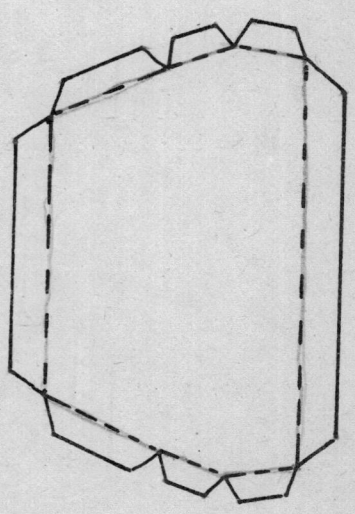

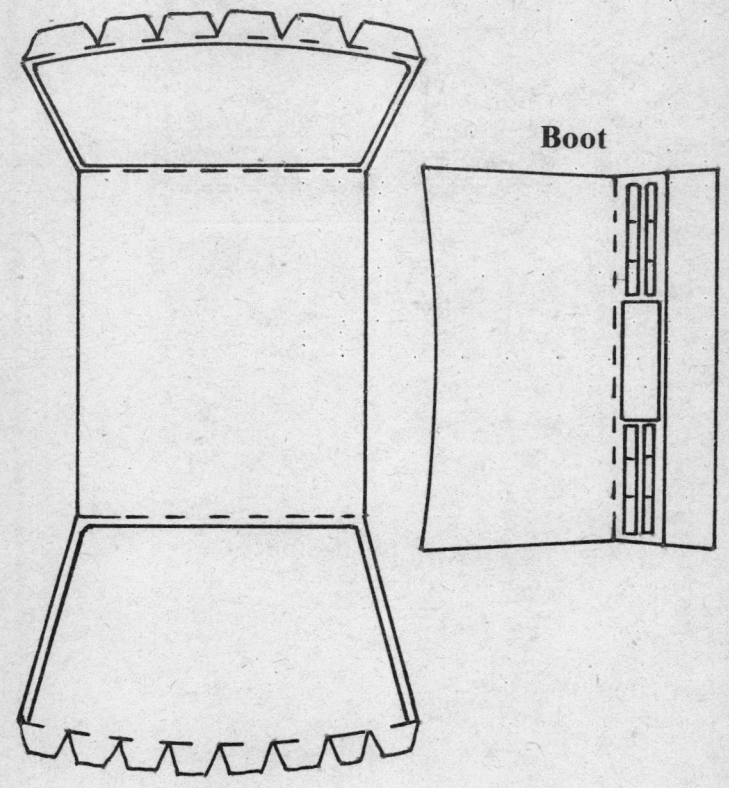

Boot

Windscreen/Roof/Rear window

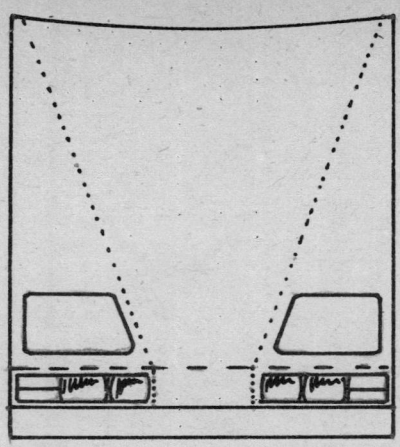

Bonnet

Tapered bonnet

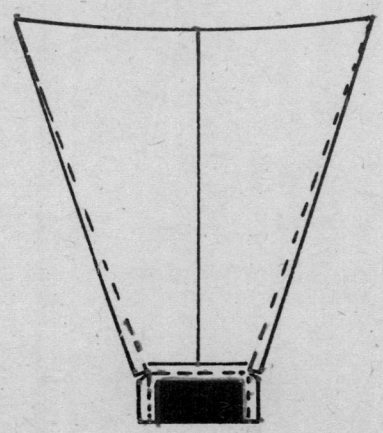

CITRÖEN

Andre Citröen was a young French engineer who set up a small factory producing a new type of double V gears before the First World War. During the war a new factory was built to produce shells and with the return of peace it was converted into a car producing plant.

The first car, the Type A, was introduced in 1919 and was built until 1926. It was the first quantity-built French car the public could afford. Citröen was the first to introduce mass production of cars to Europe. The Citröen badge is based on the original silent V gears.

The 5 CV Type C was introduced in 1922 and, in one body form, was known as the 'clover-leaf' from its seating plan of two front and one rear. A Citröen was the first car to cross the Sahara Desert.

Up until 1933, Citröen cars had been quite conventional, but then came their great technical breakthrough. They built a new front-wheel drive car with a unit construction body – there was no chassis, it being replaced by a strong body-shell. This type of construction is now used on almost every production car and certainly revolutionised the motor industry. These cars, the 11 CV and the 15 CV were ahead of their time and remained in production until 1955 when they were superceded by the equally advanced DS 19, which was built until 1975.

In the late Thirties, Citröen were developing a 'people's car' and in 1948 the 2 CV was announced. A most unusual car, it soon became popular because of its remarkable robustness, spaciousness, excellent suspension, and the way its 375 cc engine would plod along all day.

The model in this book is of the current version of the 2 CV. The car is still almost the same as it was in 1948, but the engine is larger, 602 cc, and the original corrugated bodywork has given way to normal panels. The interior

CITRÖEN 2 CV 6

fittings have also been improved. The early cars had steel tube and canvas seats. The 2 CV is cheap to buy – cheap to run (64 km.p.g. (40 m.p.g.) in typical town driving) and cheap to repair with easily detachable body panels.

The 2 CV is certainly a great success as a people's car. It fits into a class of its own and makes no attempt to compete with any other car but it has developed a unique personality that has endeared it to thousands of owners, and shows signs of going on forever, unaffected by all the modern design trends.

CITRÖEN   FRANCE

2 CV 6

Length: 3830 mm (151 ins)

Wheelbase: 2400 mm (94·5 ins)

Engine: Air cooled 2 cylinder 602 cc

Parts required:

1 Base
2 Wheel supports (plan p. 23)
2 Sides
2 Bulkheads
1 Bonnet/Windscreen
1 Rear mudguard
2 Front mudguards
4 Wheels 19 mm diameter × 5 mm
  (0·75 in × 0·2 in)
Balsa wood for bumpers and
  headlights.

Construction:

Construction of this model is basically the same as the previous ones but there are differences in the mudguards and front end.

Prepare the base and fit wheel supports at the **rear end only**. Assemble the bulkheads and sides and then the bonnet, windscreen, etc., in the usual way.

The tabs for the front wheels can now be glued to the body sides, the front end being packed out with scraps of balsa to keep them square. The mudguards should now be prepared and glued in place. Wheels, bumpers and headlights can now be fitted and the model painted.

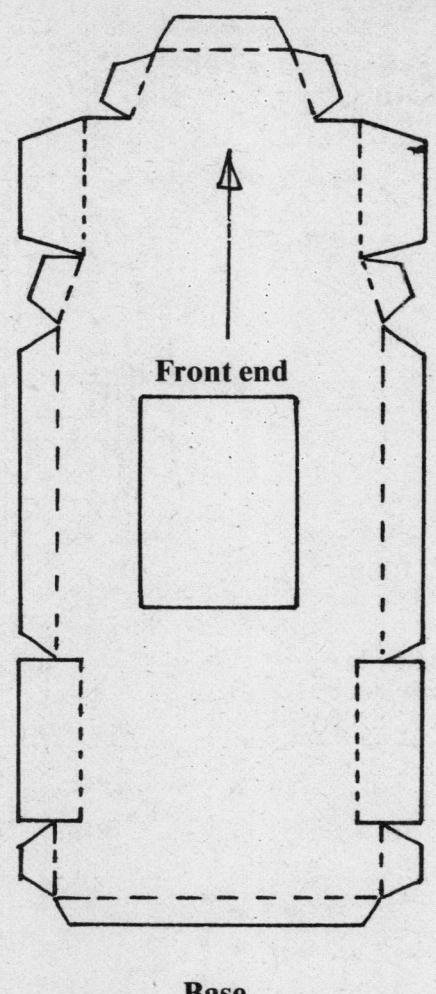

Front end

Base

**Side
(2 required)**

**Dotted lines show position
of mudguards**

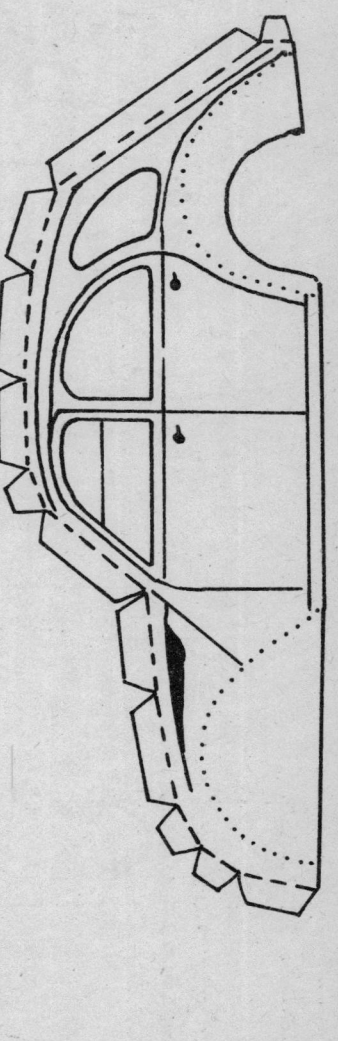

**Bulkhead
(2 required)**

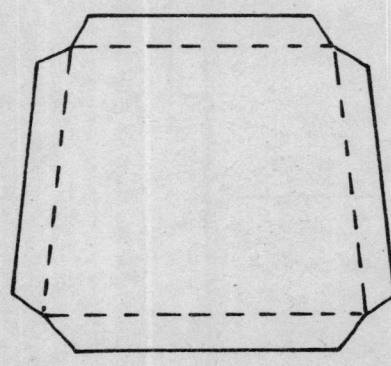

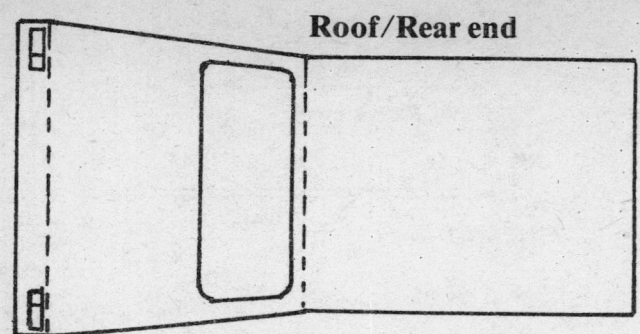

Roof/Rear end

**Front mudguard
(2 required)**

**Rear mudguard
(2 required)**

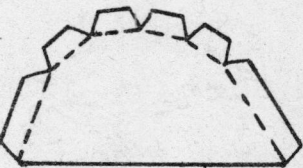

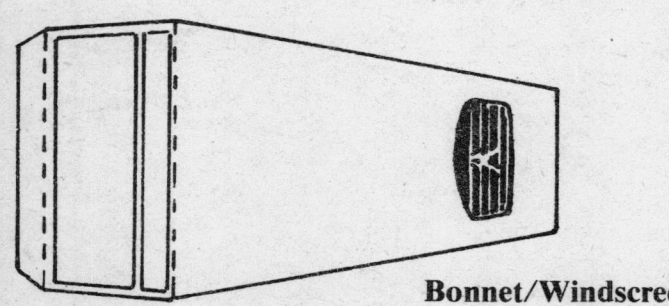

Bonnet/Windscreen

Front bumper (3 pieces)

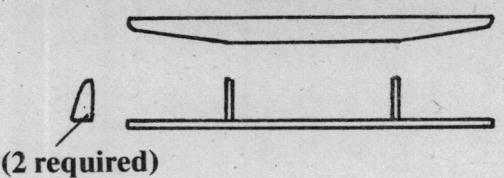

(2 required)

Assembly details

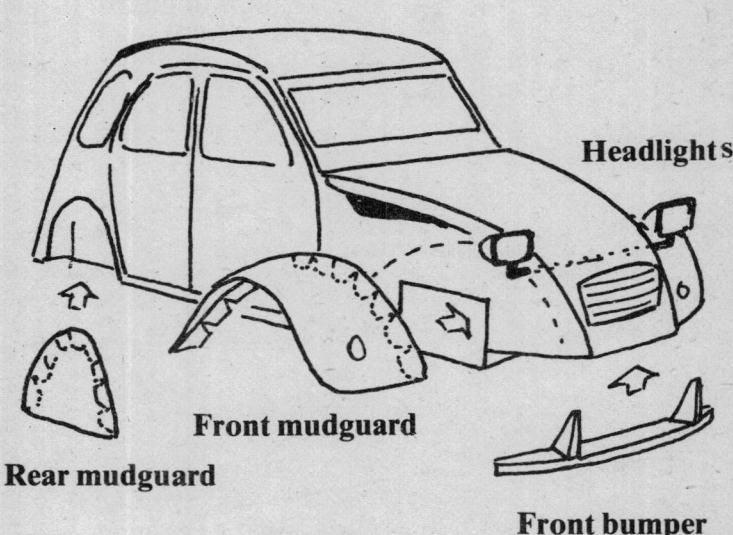

Headlights

Front mudguard

Rear mudguard

Front bumper

FIAT

F.I.A.T. are the initials of Fabbrica Italiana Automobili Torino (the Italian Motor Car Company, Turin) which was a company formed in 1898 by a group of Italian pioneers and businessmen to build motor cars. The company became the biggest Italian manufacturer and is now one of the world's major motor vehicle producers.

The first car of this company was a '3½ H.P.' with a twin cylinder 600 cc engine, three gears and two handbrakes.

All the best car makers raced in the early days and, as a result, great improvements were made to their cars. Engines became more efficient, making the cars faster; steering and brakes were developed to cope with the new power; and tyre design advanced to keep up with the larger, faster cars.

Fiat raced with considerable success in these early years and for some time were using an engine of 14 litres.

In the 1920's Fiat was the only European manufacturer using an up-to-date production policy; offering a simple, robust car that could be built in great quantities, to a large number of people. In 1936 the legendary 500 was produced. This was a very small economical car which soon became known as the 'Topolino' (little mouse) and a much developed version of this car is still in production today.

Some years ago Fiat was taken over by the Italian government and now makes vehicles ranging from small saloons to very large commercial vehicles. Motor racing continues to be supported by Fiat – the famous Ferrari sports and racing cars are built by a company which is part of the Fiat organisation.

The car chosen for this book is the Fiat X1–9. Fiat introduced this car in 1972 and it is called a 'baby Ferrari' by some people as it is an excellent mid-engined sports car. At a time when the American regulations were calling for safer cars and the world fuel crisis was developing, the X1–9 created considerable interest. It certainly was a true sports car but offered good roll-over protection, with strong bulkheads front and rear and the roll-over bar and fixed rear window giving high torsional rigidity. The 1·3 litre engine gives a lively performance with a top speed of around 100 m.p.h. (160 km.p.h.) and a fuel consumption of about 30 m.p.g. (9·2 litres 100 km).

The long nose has several good points – it gives the car a very pleasing wedge shape, it gives the front luggage compartment plenty of space (there is also a luggage boot behind the engine) and, perhaps most important of all, it is designed to absorb the impact of front end crashes, a feature essential in modern car design. The car can quickly be converted into a saloon by the fitting of a steel roof which, when not in use, stows neatly in the front boot without a loss of luggage space.

FIAT X1–9   ITALY

Length: 3844 mm (150·75 ins)

Wheelbase: 2212 mm (86·75 ins)

Engine: 4 cylinders 1290 cc
developing 73 b.h.p.

The engine is mounted behind the seats and in front of the rear axle. This layout is known as **mid-engined**.

FIAT X1-9

Parts required:

1 Base
4 Wheel supports (plan p. 23)
2 Sides
1 Bonnet/Dashboard bulkhead
1 Rear top/Seat bulkhead
1 Roll-bar
1 Seat base
4 Wheels 17 mm diameter × 5 mm
(0·7 in × 0·2 in)
Windscreen frame made from
1·5 mm ($\frac{1}{16}$ in square) wood and
bumper from strip balsa.

Construction:

1. The base and wheel supports are assembled in the usual way. The body sides are prepared and the strengthening sections are folded over and glued in place on the sides of the roll bar and the top of the doors.

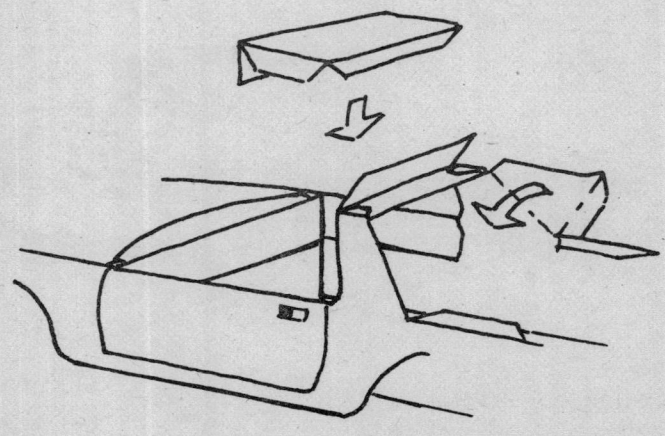

2. The sides are now attached to the base and the bonnet/bulkhead and rear top/bulkhead are glued in place to complete the basic body.

3. The seat base is prepared and glued in place. The roll-bar is completed by doubling the two halves over and glueing them together with the side tabs sandwiched between.

4. The windscreen frame is made from 1·5 mm ($\frac{1}{16}$ in square) wood cut to size and glued in place through holes in the rear corners of the bonnet. The bumpers are cut from strips of balsa 3 mm × 3 mm ($\frac{1}{8}$ in × $\frac{1}{8}$ in), sanded to shape and painted black. The front bumper is glued just below the front edge of the model, the rear bumper is in two pieces fitted either side of the number plate and below the tail lights.

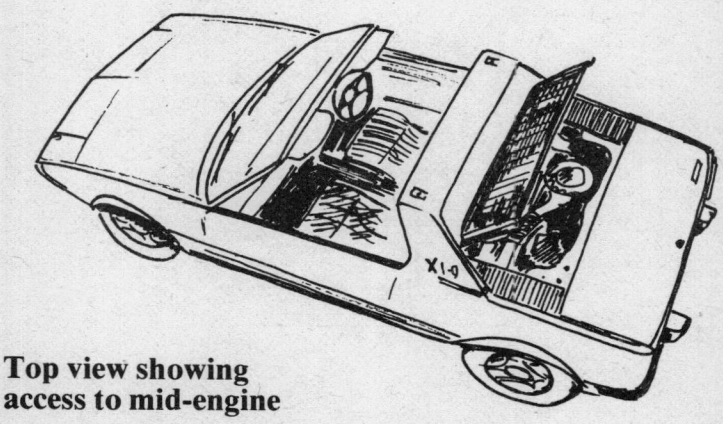

**Top view showing
access to mid-engine**

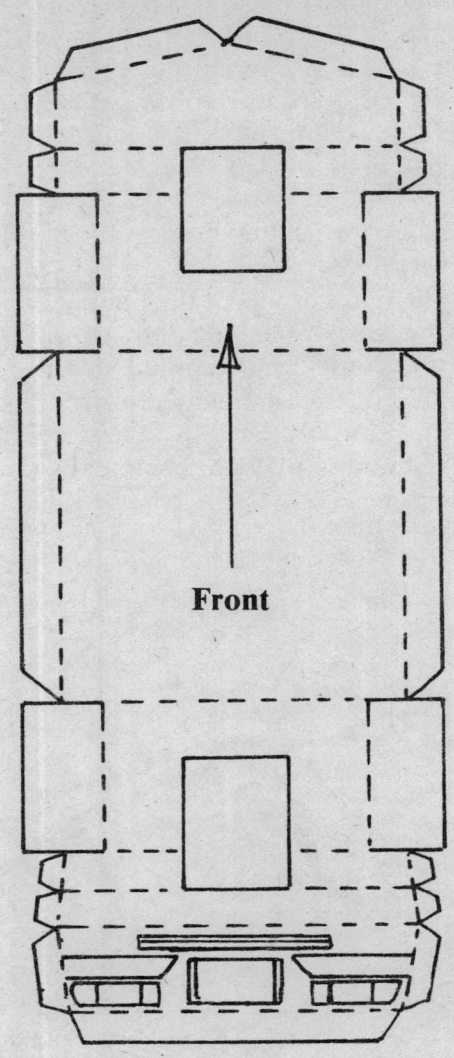

Front

Base

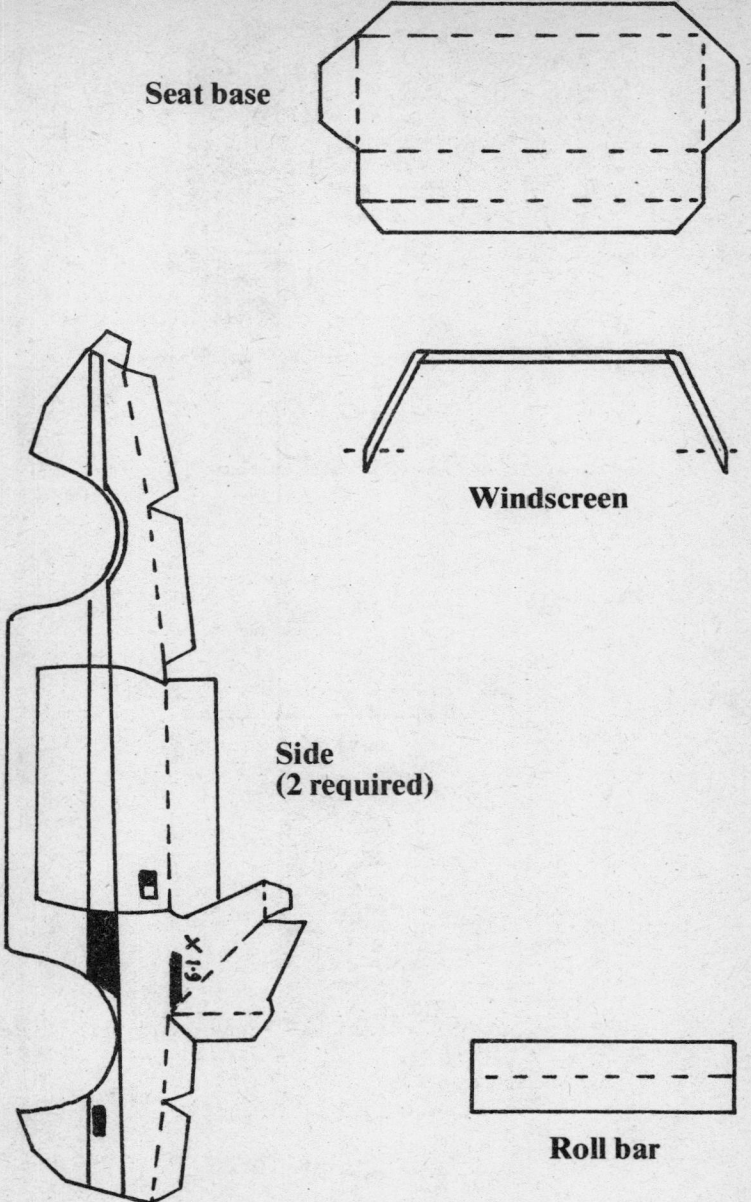

Seat base

Windscreen

**Side
(2 required)**

Roll bar

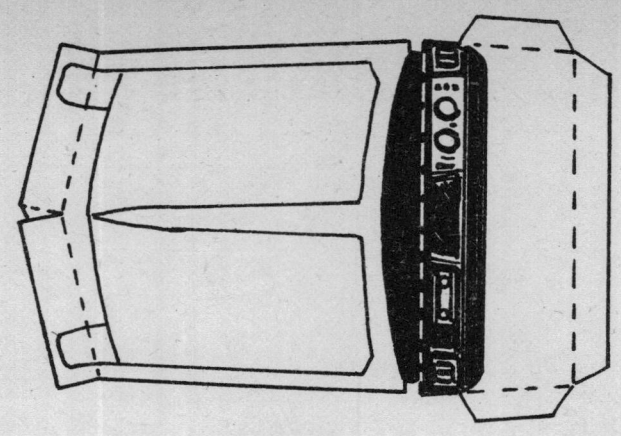

Bonnet/Dashboard bulkhead

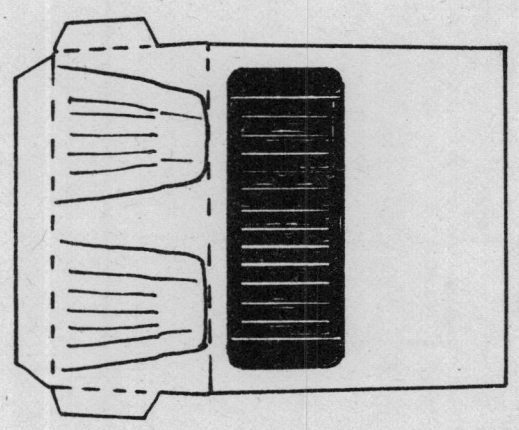

Rear top/Seat bulkhead

FERRARI

Ferrari is one of the most famous names in motor racing and expensive, high performance, sports cars.

Enzo Ferrari was born in 1898 and as a boy became interested in motor racing. His father had a business repairing cars and allowed Enzo to drive the family car when he was 13 years old. After the First World War, when he served in the Italian army as an engine fitter, he went to work for Fiat in Turin.

Ferrari drove in his first race in 1919 and in 1920 he joined Alfa Romeo as a driver and tester. During the next twelve years he had considerable success in European races. It was at this time that he adopted the now famous black prancing horse emblem. The emblem had been used by an Italian flying ace in the First World War and Ferrari painted it on a gold shield on each of the cars he drove and later on the cars made by his company.

Ferrari drove his last race in 1932 and concentrated on running his garage at Modena. He was a distributor for Alfa Romeo cars and was responsible for running the Alfa Romeo racing team until 1939.

The Ferrari factory was used for military purposes during the Second World War and was moved to Maranello in 1943. In 1946 the first racing car to bear the name Ferrari was announced, a name that was to become known throughout the world.

Ferrari's chief interest was Formula One racing and 'works teams' have contested most of the Grand Prix races over the last 30 years. Sports-racing cars have been raced by the factory and by private owners over the years with considerable success.

In the mid sixties the Ford Motor Company, keen to enter motor racing, offered to finance the Ferrari competition programme and market Ferrari production cars under the name Ford-Ferrari but the contract took

**FERRARI
512 BB BERLINETTA BOXER**

control out of Enzo Ferrari's hands, which was unaccept-
able to him, and it was not signed. Fiat came to Ferrari's
rescue with financial help and in 1969 an agreement was
signed giving Fiat a 50% holding in Ferrari and control of
production cars leaving Enzo Ferrari in charge of the
competition programme.

Ferrari production sports cars over the years have been
some of the most powerful, fast and luxurious vehicles
ever made. The model that follows is certainly all of these
things; the engine develops 380 b.h.p. and the top speed is
said to be 300 km.p.h. (188 m.p.h.).

The Berlinetta Boxer was introduced in 1971 and is a
mid-engined two-seater sports-car with roadholding,
stability and brakes to match it's outstanding
performance.

FERRARI   ITALY

512 BB BERLINETTA BOXER

Length: 4418 mm (173 ins)

Wheelbase: 2512 mm (98·5 ins)

Engine: Twelve cylinders.

4,942 cc developing 360 b.h.p.

The engine is mounted behind the
driver and in front of the rear wheels.

Parts required:

1 Base
4 Wheel supports (plan p. 23)
2 Sides
2 Bulkheads
2 Wheel arches
1 Bonnet
1 Windscreen/Roof
1 Upper rear section
4 Wheels 20 mm diameter × 6 mm
  (0·8 in × 0·25 in)

Construction:

The construction in this model (and the next one, the Pontiac Trans Am) is basically the same as the previous models.

1. Prepare and assemble the base, the sides and bulkheads in the usual way.

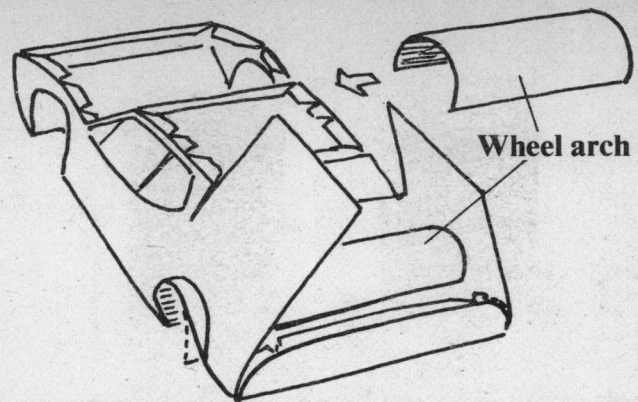

Wheel arch

2. Cut out and roll the wheel arch pieces and glue these in place as shown. The ends of these pieces protrude from the body sides and are trimmed, after fitting, to give the flared wheel arches. The dotted lines show the card that should be removed.

3. The rear body sides are now rolled over and glued in place to form the top of the vehicle and then the triangular pieces are added. These are in one piece, the rectangular part is glued centrally to the rear of the car with the inside triangular section glued to the inside of the tab at the rear of the side windows. The outside triangular piece is then folded down and glued in place.

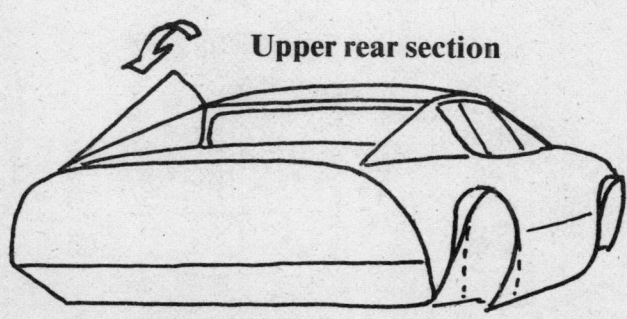

Upper rear section

The bonnet, windscreen and roof can now be added to finish the model in the usual way.

Plans

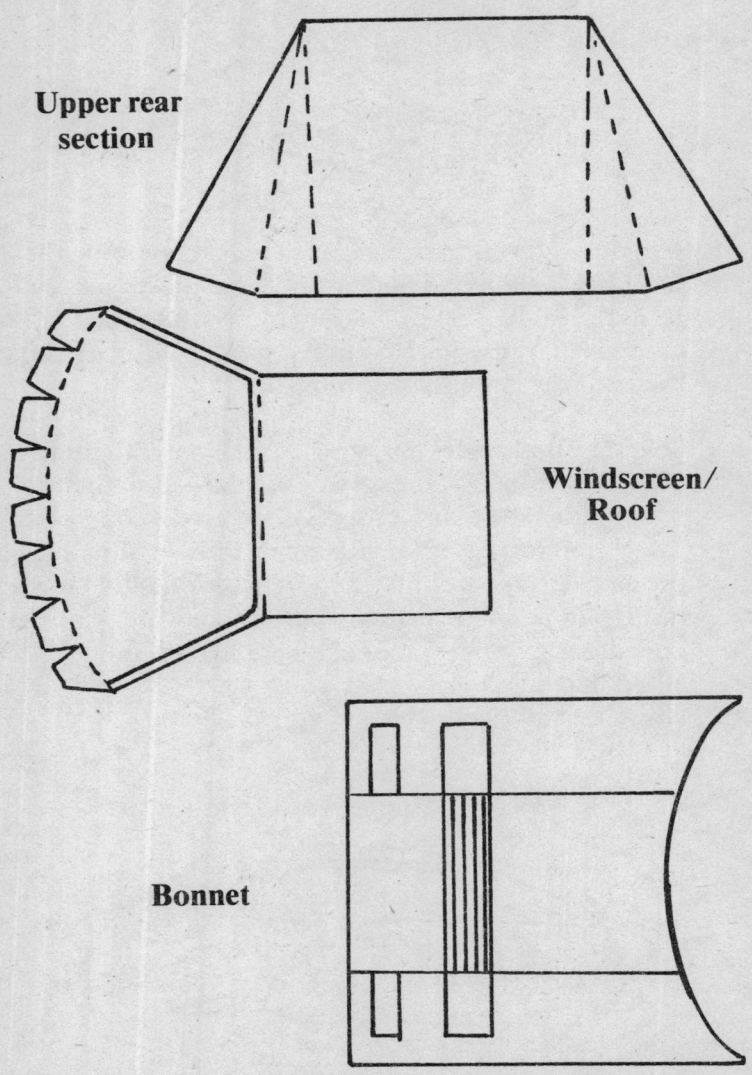

Upper rear
section

Windscreen/
Roof

Bonnet

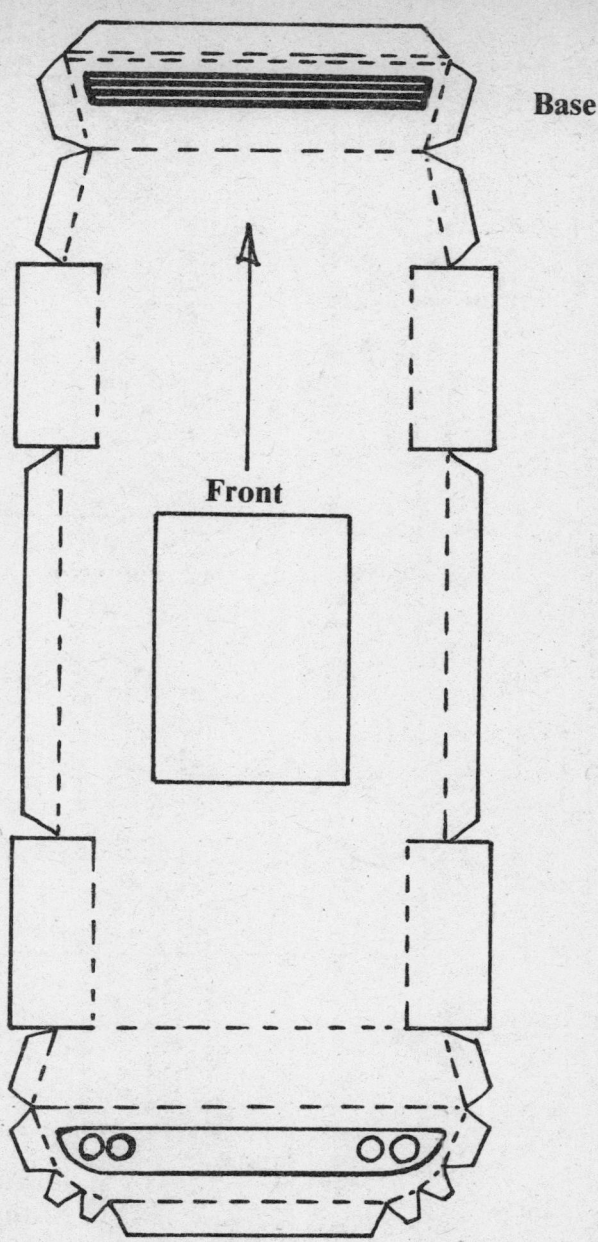

Base

Front

69

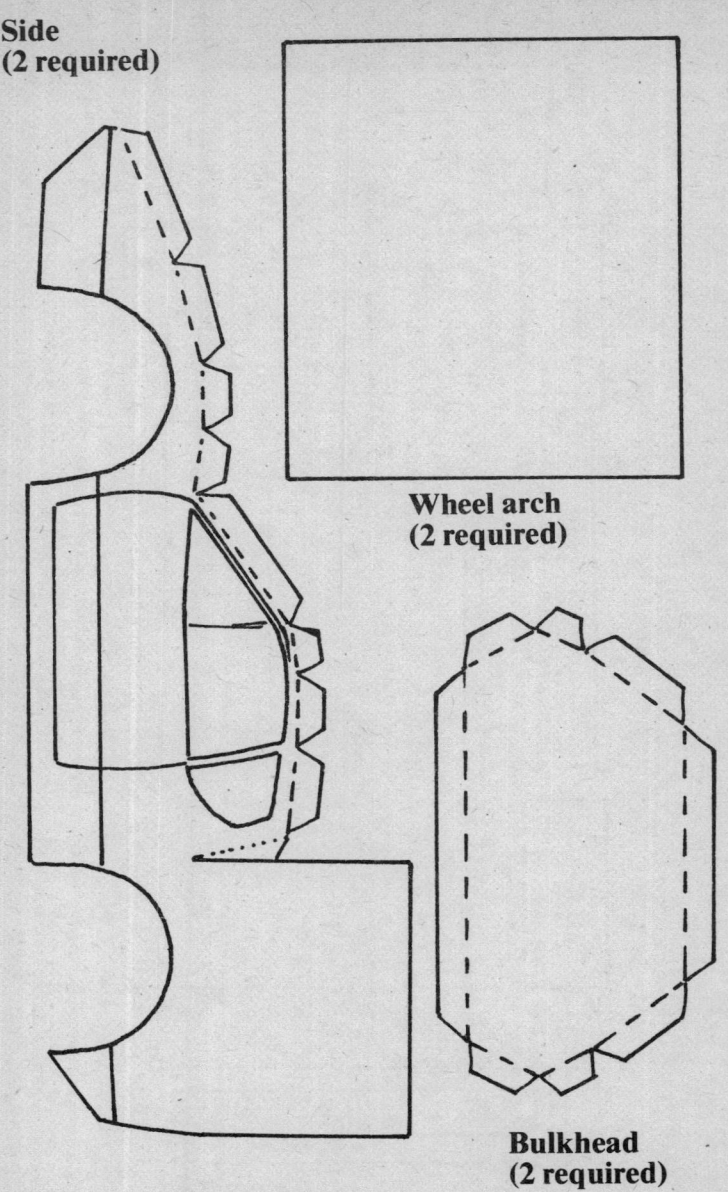

Side
(2 required)

Wheel arch
(2 required)

Bulkhead
(2 required)

PONTIAC

In 1893 Edward Murphy founded the Pontiac Buggy Company in the town of Pontiac, Michigan. The name of the town was taken from a mighty Indian Chief of the eighteenth century. In 1907 Murphy started making motor cars but he dropped the original name and called them Oakland, a name which was used until 1931.

General Motors took over Oakland in 1925 and produced a new model for 1926 which they called the Pontiac; a low-priced six cylinder car. The Pontiac proved very popular and as new models were introduced the Oakland was phased out. The first Pontiac was advertised as *The Chief of the Sixes* and for many years the bonnet motif was an Indian warrior in ceremonial head-dress.

All the marques produced by General Motors were established manufacturers taken over by the company (except Pontiac which they introduced) and their activities are not confined to the United States. In England, Vauxhall/Bedford, and in Germany, Opel, are part of the General Motors Empire and both are controlled from America.

In the mid 1950s Pontiac designed motor cars to cultivate the currently fashionable 'youth image' and set the pattern for the styles of the sixties with simpler lines and less chrome. During the sixties, the Pontiac range included the G.T.O. which had a new, large, powerful engine and was the first of the 'muscle cars'.

In January 1967, the Firebird was announced. This is the subject of the next model and, from its introduction, has been Pontiac's classic performance car. Various engines are available from the 105 b.h.p. V6 to the 185 b.h.p. V8. The most powerful version is known as the Pontiac Firebird Trans Am. By European standards it is a large car and the seating is 2 + 2 which means that there are two good size front seats and two smaller seats in the back which is common in high performance sports cars.

PONTIAC   U.S.A.

FIREBIRD TRANS AM.

Length: 5024 mm (197 ins)

Wheelbase: 2754 mm (108 ins)

Engine: **V8** 6,609 cc
                developing 185 b.h.p.

Parts required:

1 Base (made from 2 pieces)
4 Wheel supports (plan p. 23)
2 Sides
2 Bulkheads
2 Wheel arches (from Ferrari plans)
1 Headlight bulkhead
1 Taillight bulkhead
1 Bonnet
1 Air intake
1 Windscreen/Roof
1 Rear window
1 Rear spoiler
4 Wheels 20 mm diameter × 6 mm
   (0·8 in × 0·25 in)

PONTIAC FIREBIRD TRANS AM.

Construction:

The basic construction of this model is similar to the Ferrari but several parts are different.

1. The front of the base is folded to make the front bumper and the headlight bulkhead is fitted before the bonnet is glued in place. The lip on the front of the bonnet is rolled down and glued to the top of the bumper.

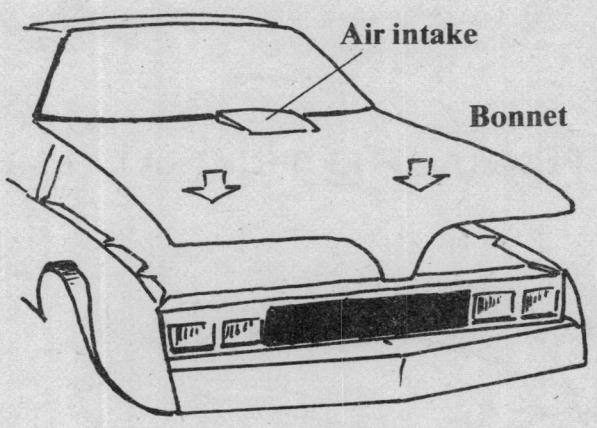

The air intake is glued to the top of the bonnet in the position shown.

2. The rear of the base makes the rear bumper and the taillight bulkhead is fitted before the rear body sections are joined to make the boot lid. The spoiler is glued to the rear edge of the finished boot.

The rear window is glued to the tabs on the back of the roof, behind the side windows and to the top of the boot.

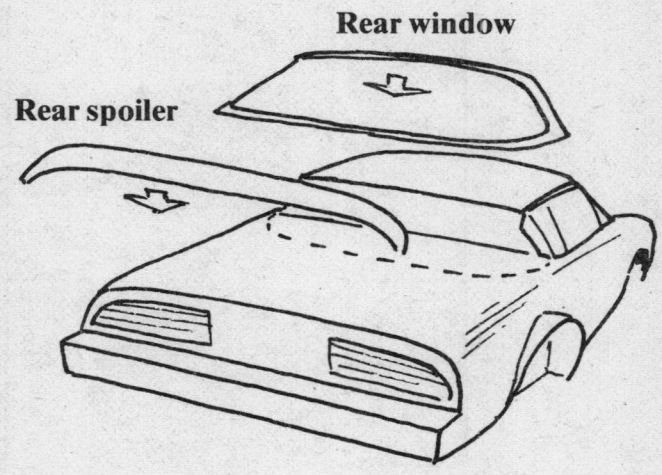

Rear window

Rear spoiler

Plans

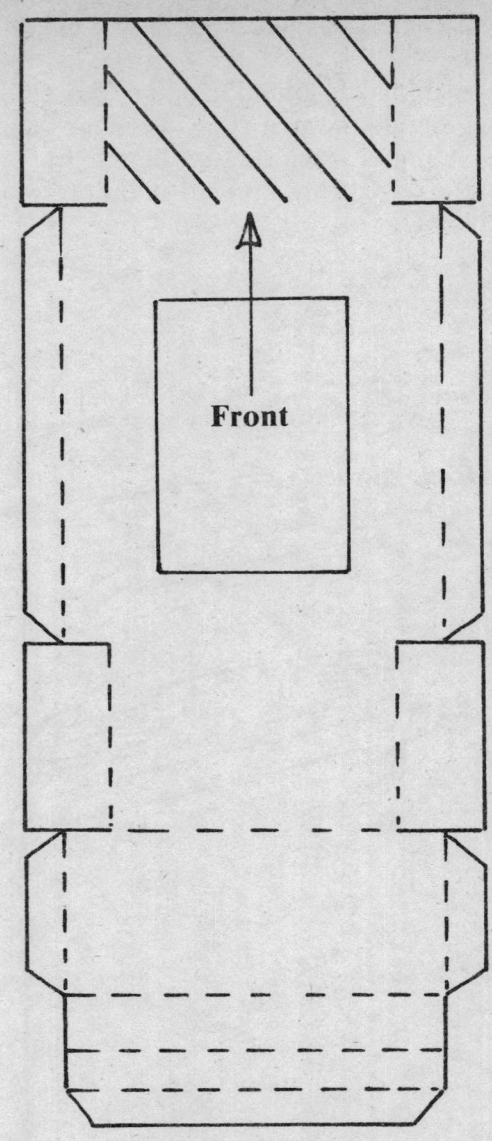

Front

Base

(Add base front, overlapping shaded areas)

**Side
(2 required)**

**Bulkhead
(2 required)**

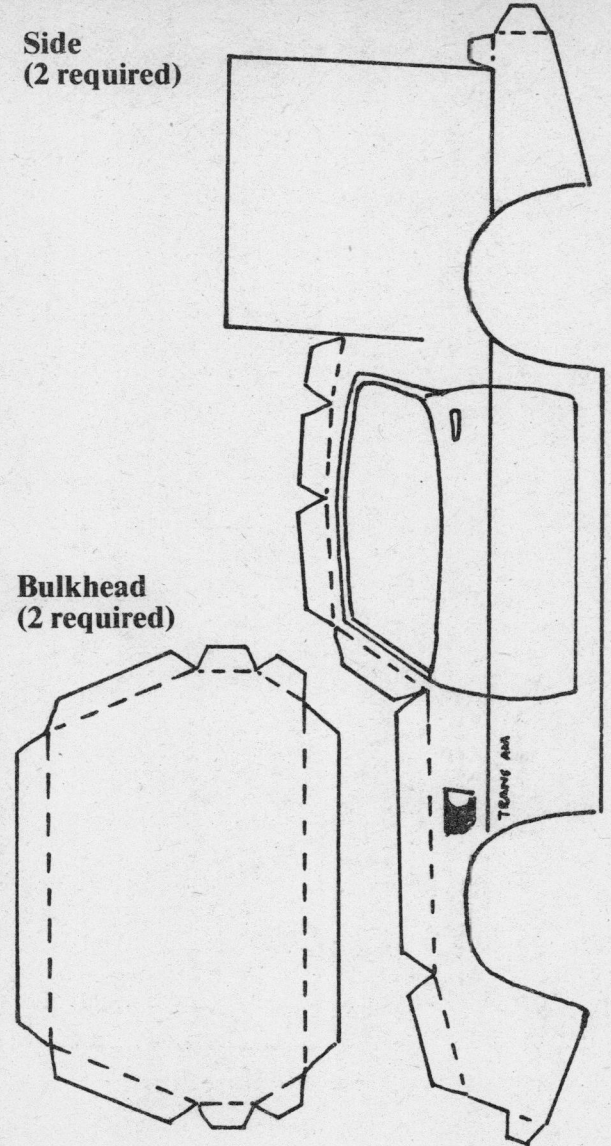

TRANS AM

Bonnet

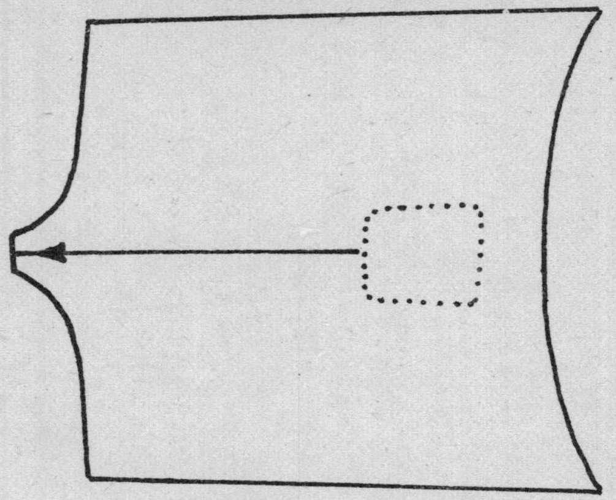

Air intake

Headlight bulkhead

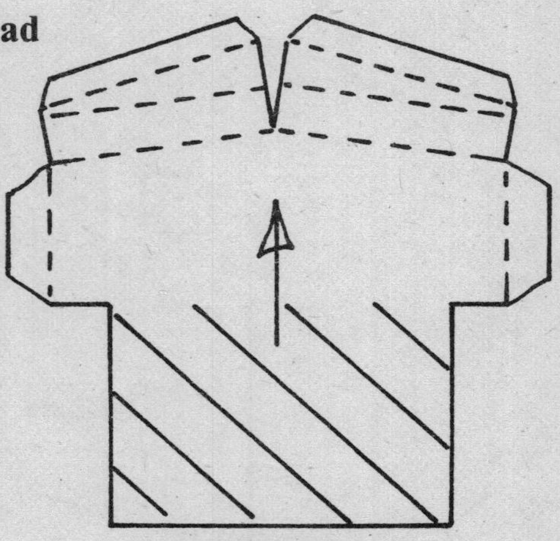

Base front

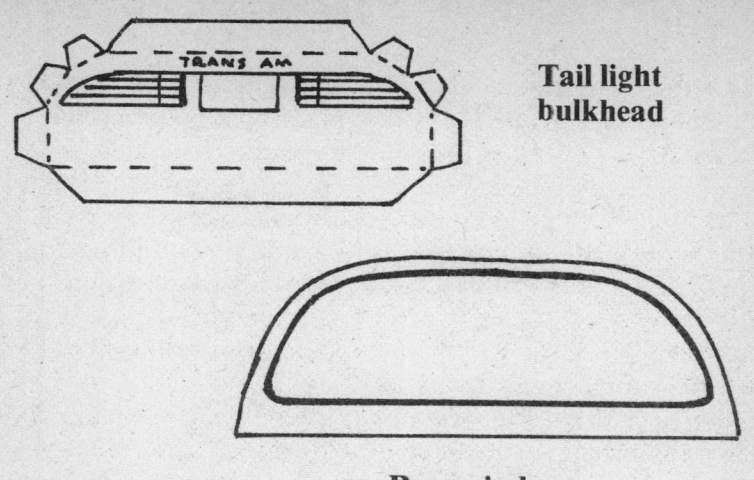

Tail light bulkhead

Rear window

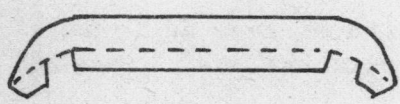

Rear spoiler

Windscreen/Roof

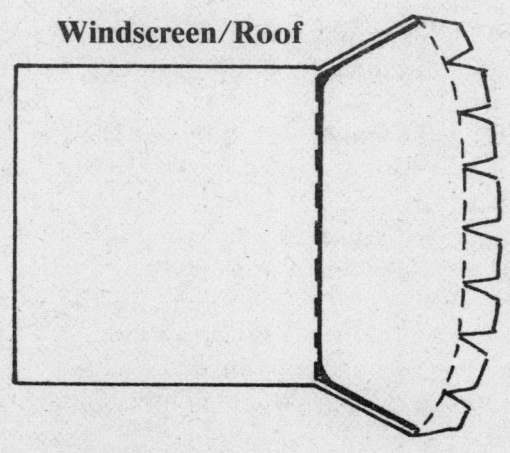

79

LOTUS

Colin Chapman started his motor industry career dealing in second-hand cars. He also took an active part in motor sport with home-made 'specials' and achieved a great deal of success as his cars had tremendous performance and roadholding. There was an obvious market for cars of this type and Chapman set up a factory to build his first 'production car' the Lotus 6. For many years would-be owners could buy their cars in kit form and assemble them at home, avoiding purchase-tax and, as a result, making the car much cheaper.

In 1957 the Lotus Seven was introduced, this car was very light, had excellent roadholding and, depending on the engine used, was very fast. This car has been very competitive in club racing since it was first made and is still in production since Lotus sold the whole project to a South London garage.

Since the mid fifties Lotus have been racing Formula 1 cars, and have some of the best grand-prix cars which have been very successful. Perhaps the best known of these is the black and gold 'John Player Special'.

1957 saw the production of the first true road car, the Lotus Elite. This was a very attractive, sleek sports coupe built in fibreglass which made it strong and light and remarkably economical for a car of this type. The cost of producing the fibre-glass body became prohibitive and very soon the Elite was replaced by the Elan which had a steel chassis and could be produced as an open sports car.

In 1966 the Elan gave way to the Europa. Lotus signed an agreement with Renault for the supply of modifed engine/transmissions for the new car, one of the first quantity produced mid engined cars in the world. This car again was a great success and was originally sold by Renault dealers throughout Europe.

In the 1970's Lotus became producers of refined, high

performance grand touring cars in competition with the manufacturers of the world's best high performance, prestige cars. The new Elite, the Eclat and the Esprit are the three models in the range. All three share the same mechanical components, the Elite and the Eclat have the engine in the front but the Esprit continues the Europa and racing car pattern of mid-engine layout. The first two cars are both four seaters whereas the Esprit has just two seats.

The following model is of the Lotus Esprit. The exotic body of this two seat, mid-engined, high performance sports car was designed by one of the world's leading stylists, Georgeto Giugiaro, and lives up to the claim that it is 'Today's Car designed for Tomorrow'. It has a top speed of nearly 230 km.p.h (140 m.p.h.) and yet is more economical than many family saloons.

This is the car made famous by James Bond in the film *Live and Let Die*. Production Esprits were modified and filmed performing some amazing feats including an underwater scene where the car transformed itself into a submarine.

LOTUS ESPRIT   ENGLAND

Length: 4207 mm (165 ins)

Wheelbase: 2448 mm (96 ins)

Engine: 4 cylinder 1973 cc
             developing 160 b.h.p.

Parts required:

1 Base
4 Wheel supports (plan p. 23)
2 Sides
2 Bulkheads
1 Bonnet
1 Windscreen/Roof/Rear
4 Wheels 19 mm diameter × 6 mm
  (0·74 in × 0·25 in)
Bumpers from balsa strip

Construction:

Construction of this model is again quite straightforward.
The base, at the rear, includes the back end of the car
which should be assembled, like the Ferrari, to form a
false boot onto which the rear window and sides are
attached.

LOTUS ESPRIT

Plans

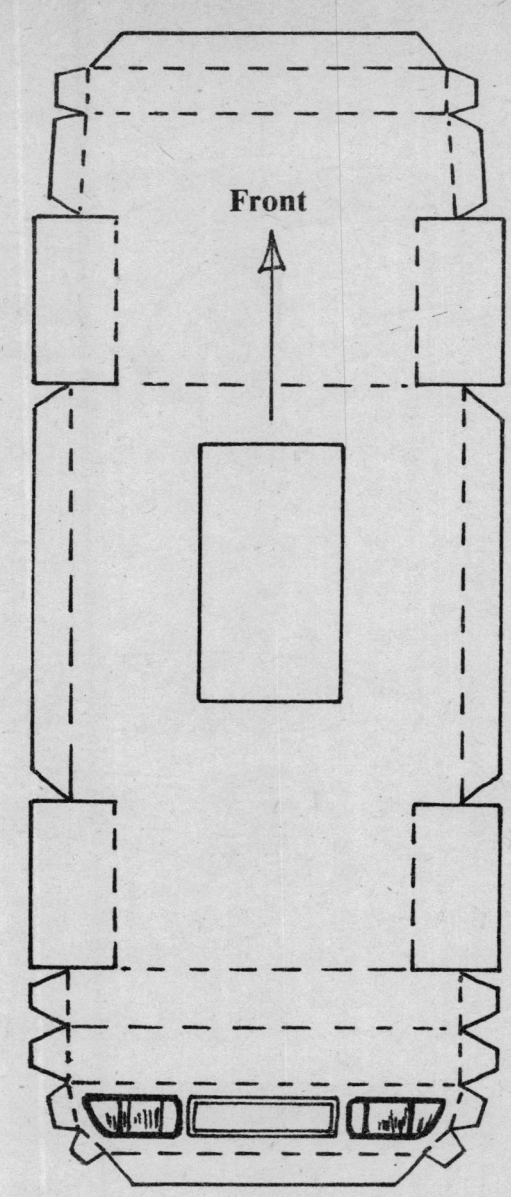

Front

Base

**Bulkhead
(2 required)**

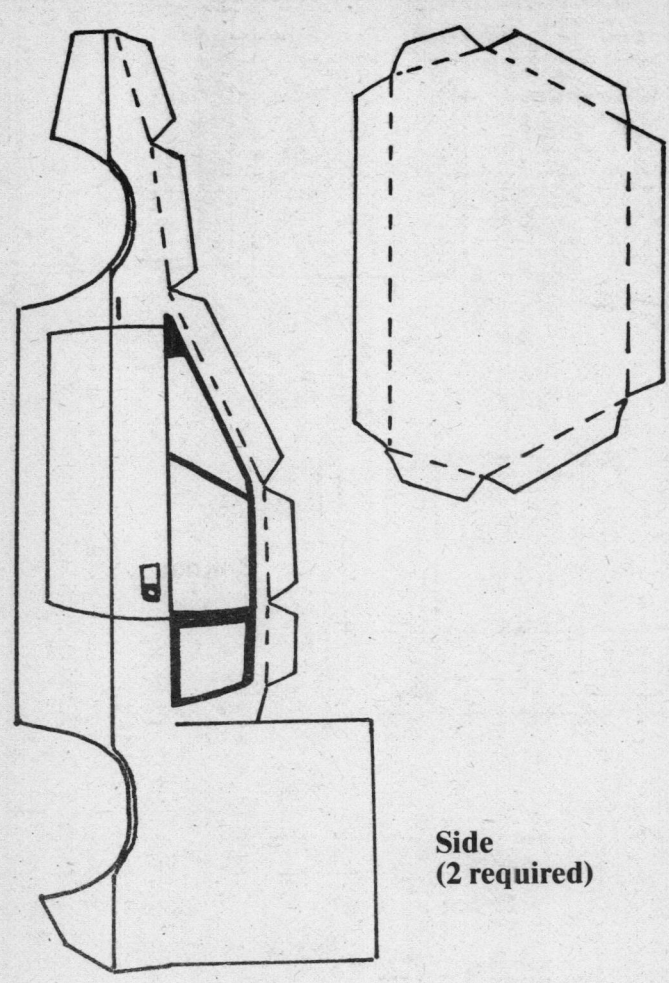

**Side
(2 required)**

Windscreen/Roof/Rear end

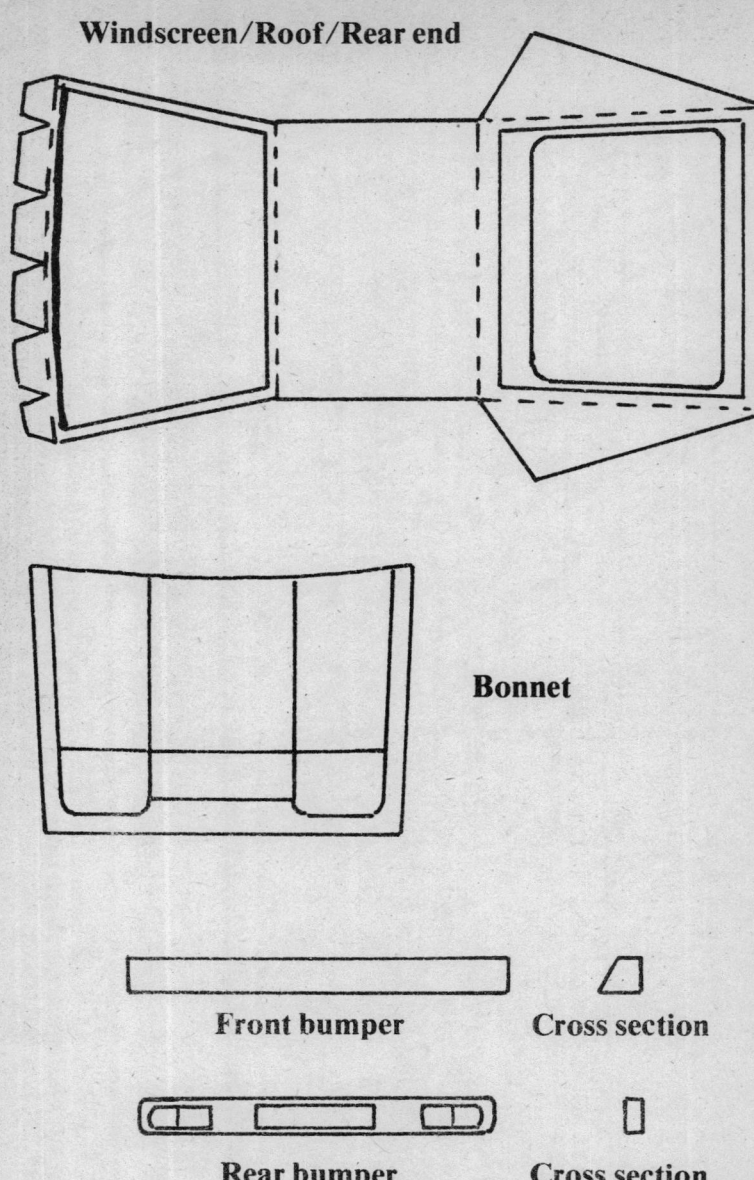

Bonnet

Front bumper

Cross section

Rear bumper

Cross section

MERCEDES

In the 1880's a German engineer, Gottlieb Daimler was involved in the development of the internal combustion engine. In 1885 he built the world's first motor cycle and his first car the following year but the business was principally concerned with building engines for other vehicle manufacturers.

The first production Daimler cars were built in 1896 and very soon after this cars were built under licence in England where the marque became one of the most famous of all. The last German Daimler was built in 1902. In 1901 a wealthy customer ordered a number of cars to his own requirements. These new cars were designed by Wilhelm Maybach. They were to a completely new design and are considered to be the forerunner of modern designs. They had pressed steel chassis considerably lower than usual and the position of engine, radiator, etc., was basically the same as we know it today.

The customer who ordered these new cars, Emil Jellinek, felt that the name Daimler was not suitable and he persuaded the company to give his cars a new name. The cars were called after his daughter Mercedes but by 1902, all production cars adopted the new name and the German Daimler was no more. In 1926 Mercedes merged with Benz and the Mercedes Benz was produced.

Mercedes were involved in racing from 1901 and were very successful, quickly gaining a reputation as producers of really fast quality cars.

The model that follows is of the Mercedes which won the 1924 Targa Florio Race. Paul Daimler built three cars for the 1923 Indianapolis 500 mile race and during the following winter the design was modified in detail by Dr. Ferdinand Porsche, who had joined the company as chief engineer. The three cars entered the race and finished 1st, 10th and 15th. The engine was small by Mercedes

Converted for road use

1924 'TARGA FLORIO' MERCEDES

Stripped for racing

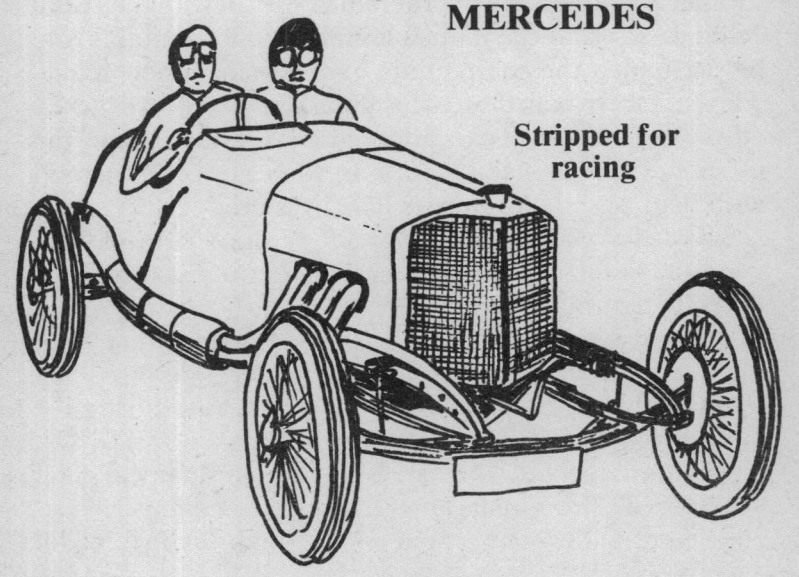

standards, 2 litres, but it was supercharged and produced 120 b.h.p. giving a top speed of about 185 km.p.h. (115 m.p.h.).

The traditional colour of Mercedes racing cars was white and a great number of production cars were painted the same way. In the late twenties and thirties, Mercedes Benz developed a series of very fast and impressive supercharged sports cars, large luxurious saloons and drophead coach built vehicles for ceremonial use and selected important private owners.

In the 1950s Mercedes Benz re-entered motor racing and dominated the circuits for several years with Fangio and Stirling Moss as main drivers.

MERCEDES   GERMANY

1924 'TARGA FLORIO' MERCEDES

Length: 3723 mm (146 ins)

Wheelbase: 2741 mm (107·5 ins)

Engine: 4 cylinder 2 litres
developing 68 b.h.p. or 120 b.h.p.
when supercharged.

Parts required:

1 Balsa base
  120 mm × 32 mm × 5 mm
  ($4\frac{3}{4}$ ins × $1\frac{1}{4}$ ins × $\frac{1}{36}$ in)
1 Dashboard bulkhead
1 Body front
1 Radiator
2 Rear bulkheads
1 Rear body
2 Axles 1·5 mm diameter ($\frac{1}{16}$ in) dowel
  48 mm long (1·9 ins)
5 Wheels 24 mm diameter × 4 mm
  (0·95 in × 0·15 in)
  Drinking straw for exhaust.

Construction:

This model and the three that follow are a little different
from the previous ones. The original cars were built on
separate chasses with exposed axles and the models are
similar. The base is replaced by a balsa chassis and the
axles are made from 1·5 mm ($\frac{1}{16}$ in) dowel (or cocktail
sticks).

1. The first step is to make the balsa base.

Mark out the wood with carbon paper and a
compass point as before, or transfer the plan by
measuring the lines.

Carefully cut out the balsa chassis with a sharp
craft knife and a ruler. Be sure to keep the knife
upright so that the edges of the wood will be square.

Base

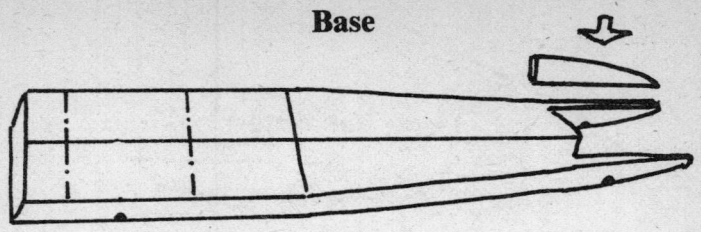

2. Mark out the axle positions and other details on the chassis and trim the front end as shown to represent the original chassis and springs.

3. Cut out the dashboard bulkhead and body front section in the usual way. Glue the bulkhead to the chassis in the correct position and then attach the body section as shown, the lower edge of the rear half is glued to the lower edge of the chassis and the short piece at the front end is fitted, but not glued, above the wood. Cut out and fit the radiator into the front of the bonnet. The pieces of card below each side of the model should now be rolled under the chassis and the ends glued together on a piece of 5 mm ($\frac{3}{16}$ in) balsa to make the under shield.

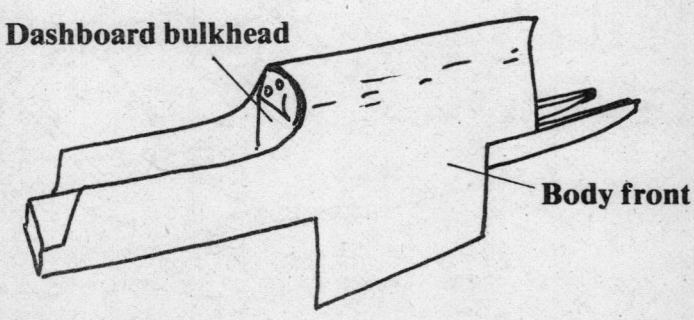

Dashboard bulkhead

Body front

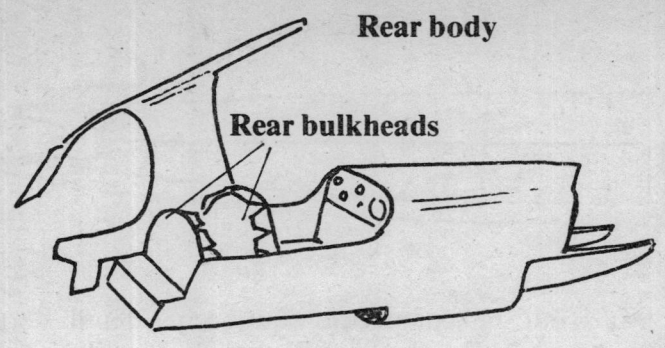

Rear body

Rear bulkheads

4. Cut out the two rear bulkheads and glue in place between the sides already in place. Cut out the body rear section and mount as shown – the bottom edge of each side to the lower edge of the chassis and the front edge adjoining the rear of the under body shield. The two rear pieces are rolled round and mounted to the back of the chassis to make the spare wheel compartment.

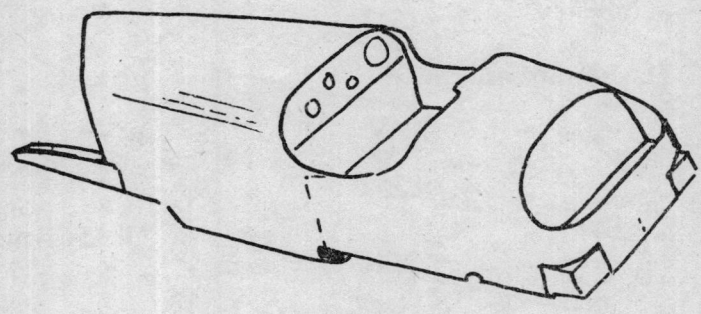

5. Cut the axles to length and glue in place.

   You will need five wheels and they need a hole in the centre to fix them to the axle. The spare wheel must be cut down to fit into the compartment. Glue the road wheels to the axles and make sure that the model sits correctly on a flat surface.

   The exhaust system is made from drinking straws as shown and glued in place.

Most of these older cars have open cockpits and should be fitted with a steering wheel. In each case they are about 13 mm ($\frac{1}{2}$ in) diameter and can best be made by cutting a disc of perspex or card to size and painting on the wheel rim and spokes. The wheel can then be glued to a short length of dowel and mounted in place.

The model should be painted white. This was the colour used for almost all German racing cars and was very popular with buyers of the pre-war Mercedes sports cars.

Plans

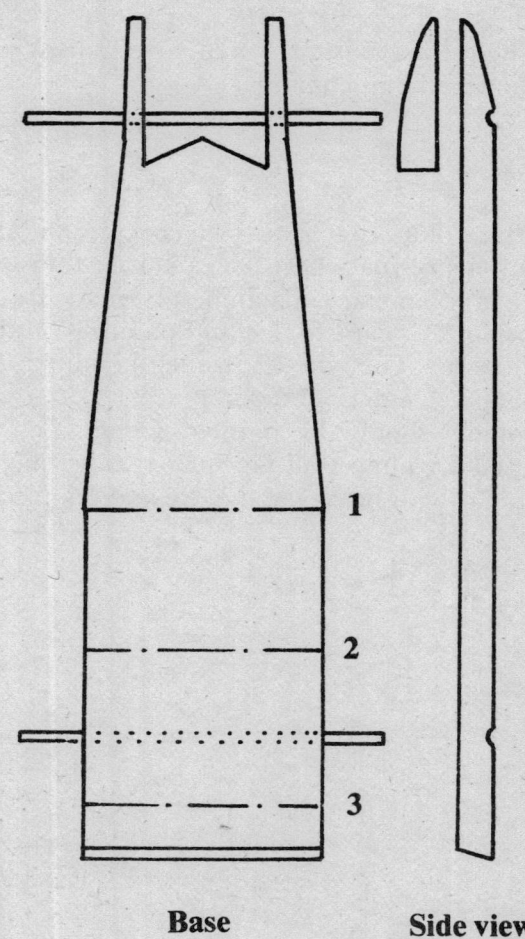

1

2

3

Base   **Side view**

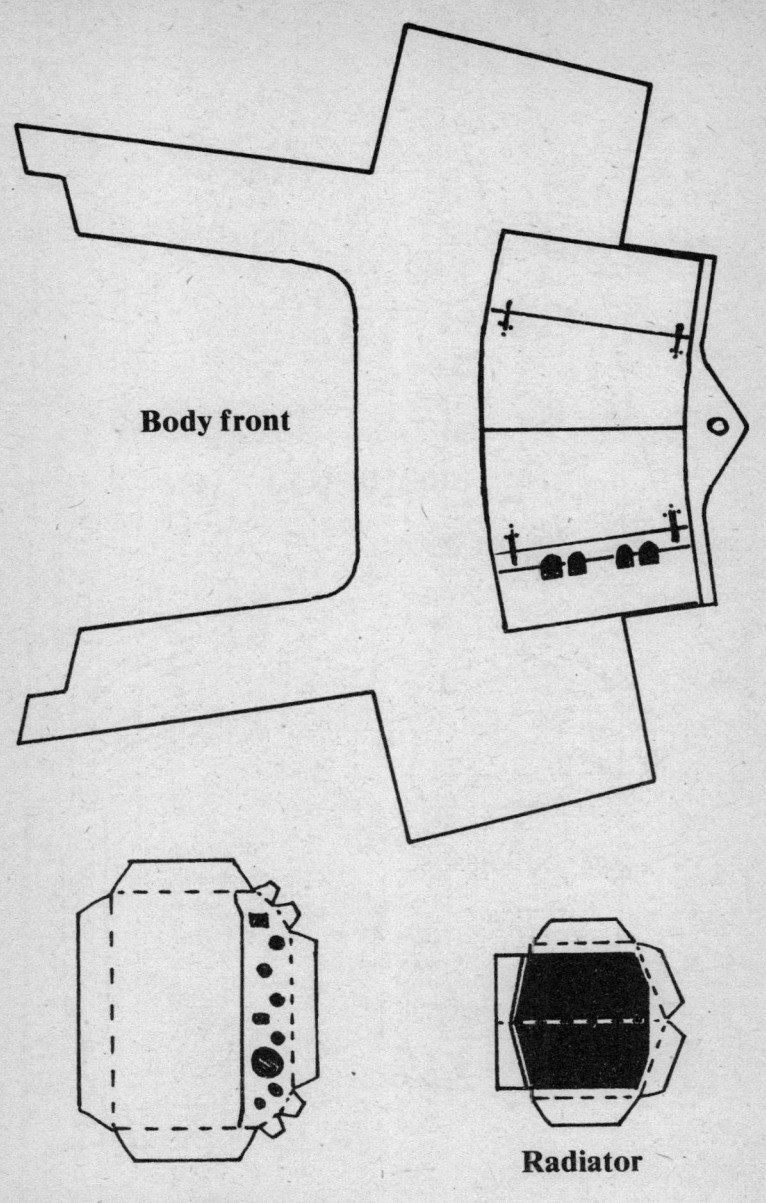

Body front

Dashboard bulkhead — 1

Radiator

95

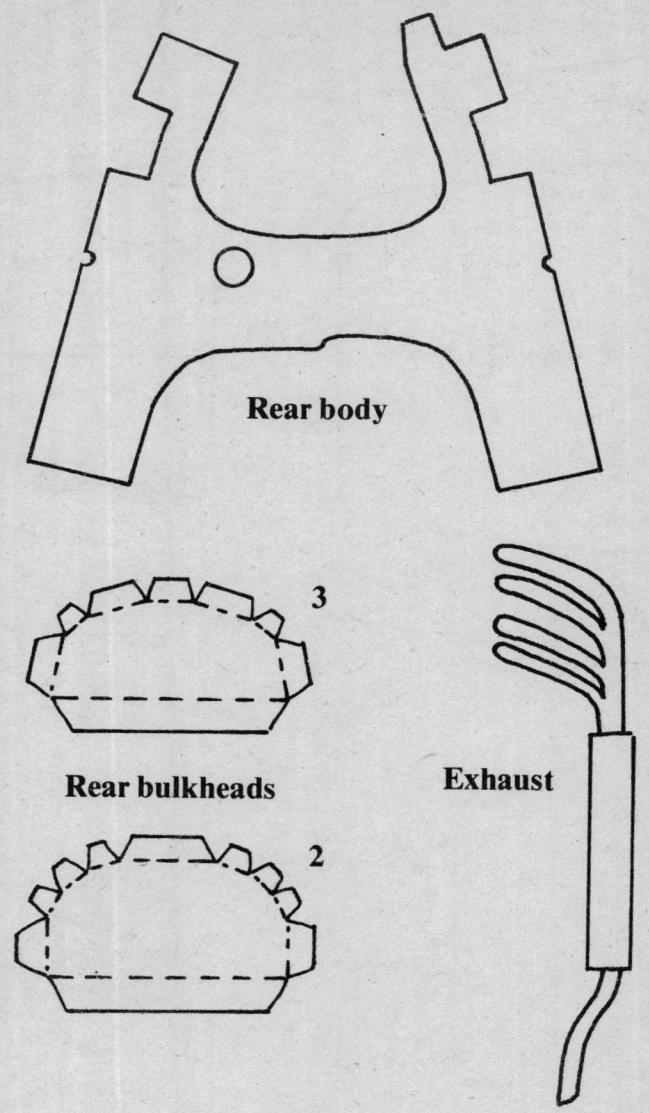

Rear body

Rear bulkheads

3

2

Exhaust

BUGATTI

Ettore Bugatti was born in 1881. He was the son of an artist and certainly had a good eye for mechanical beauty. He was one of the last engineer-artists in a world which was rapidly being changed by scientific knowledge and technology.

Bugatti designed his first car when only eighteen and sold a licence to build his second before he was twenty-one. He sold several designs over the next few years and then set up his own factory at Molsheim in 1910. For the next 37 years, until his death in 1947, Bugatti produced an amazing number of racing, sports and grand touring cars, as well as engines for aeroplanes, rail cars and boats.

Bugatti built cars for royalty which were large and extremely elegant; he built saloon cars that combined luxury with excellent performance; he built sports cars and developed a whole series of racing cars that dominated the racing circuits in the pre-war years.

Cars built by Bugatti have, for many years, been collectors' items. Many are kept in museums and car collections but a great number still compete in vintage car races and their owners meet regularly in the Bugatti Owners Club.

Each car in the Bugatti range was identified by a number and the model in this book is of the Type 59. This car was designed at the end of 1933 to be raced the following year and was the last of a series of great grand-prix cars built at Molsheim.

The Type 59 was not the most successful Bugatti racing car but it did win many races in the years up to the outbreak of war. In 1936 Earl Howe lapped the outer circuit of Brooklands at 232 km.p.h. (138·34 m.p.h.) and in 1937 Wimille, after winning several grand prix races, won the 400,000 franc prize for the 270 km (162 mile) race on the 20 km (12 mile) road circuit at Montlhery at the incredible average speed of 152 km.p.h. (91·13 m.p.h.).

BUGATTI   **FRANCE**

TYPE 59   1934

Length: 3840 mm (150·5 ins)

Wheelbase: 2600 mm (102 ins)

Engine: 6 cylinder 3·3 litre developing 230 b.h.p.

Several other engines were used at this time with capacities of 3·8, 4·7 and 4·9 litres.

BUGATTI 1934 TYPE 59

Parts required:

1 Balsa base 116 mm × 26 mm × 5 mm
  ($4\frac{3}{4}$ ins × $1\frac{1}{16}$ ins × $\frac{3}{16}$ in)
1 Dashboard bulkhead
1 Radiator
1 Body front
1 Seat bulkhead
1 Body rear
4 Wheels 23 mm diameter × 5 mm
  (0·95 in × 0·2 in)
Axles from 1·5 mm diameter ($\frac{1}{16}$ in)
dowel 44 mm long ($1\frac{3}{4}$ ins)
Exhaust pipe from drinking straw

Construction:

This model is built in the same way as the Mercedes and should not prove difficult.

The exhaust system should be made from a thin drinking straw glued in place, the petrol filler caps behind the seat from small lengths of dowel and the small screen from a scrap of perspex 18 mm × 5 mm ($\frac{5}{16}$ in × $\frac{3}{16}$ in) with the top corners rounded.

The traditional colour for French racing cars is blue and most Bugattis were painted this colour.

Plans

Side view showing position of other parts

Base

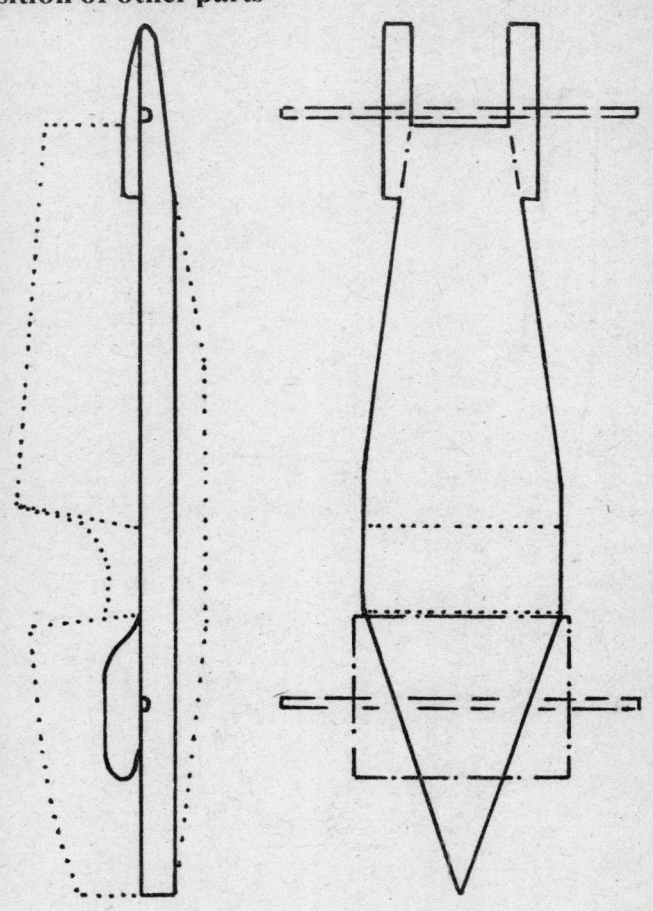

(Chain dotted section glued in place to represent rear chassis, springs, etc.)

Body front

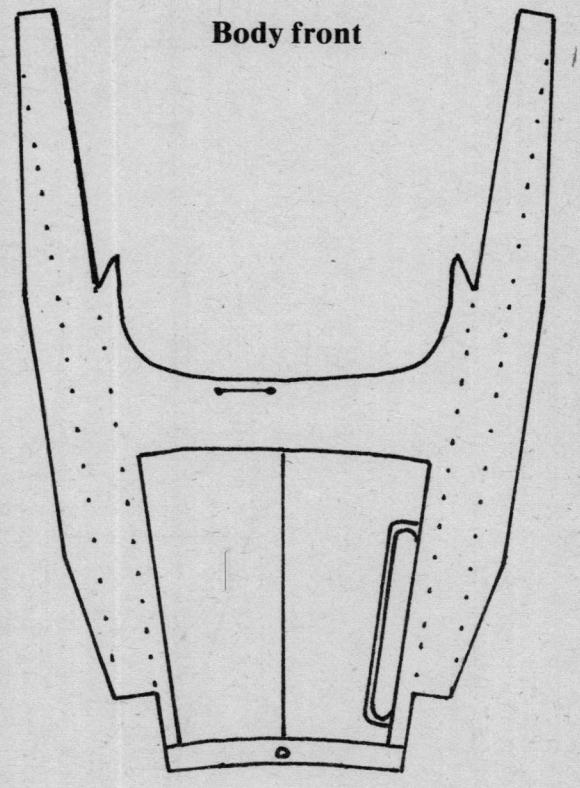

(Dotted lines show position of base)

Body rear

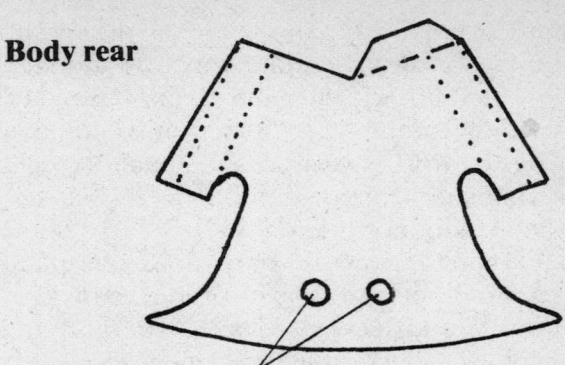

Petrol caps

Seat bulkhead — 2

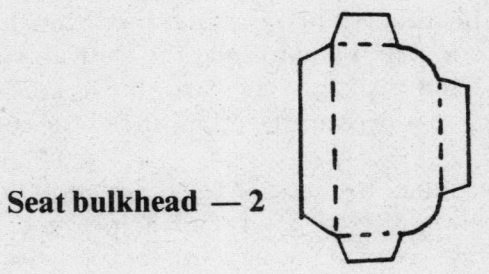

Radiator

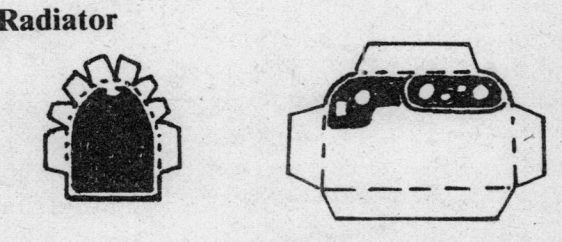

Dashboard bulkhead — 1

FORD

The Ford Motor Company is one of the world's major motor manufacturing empires and its founder, Henry Ford, was perhaps the most important figure of all in the history of the motor car. Ford gained his mechanical knowledge by working with clocks, machine tools, marine engineering and steam engines.

In 1888 Henry Ford took a small isolated house and set up a workshop to spend his spare time experimenting and building prototypes. In 1896 he produced his first vehicle, a quadricycle, and decided to leave his job and concentrate on his motor car. Over the next few years he lost a lot of money developing his ideas and testing them in racing machines.

About this time Henry Ford scraped together all the money he could find and formed the Detroit Automobile Company, but by 1900 he was in serious financial difficulties and it became necessary to sell the company to pay his debts.

Ford continued to race his machines and after a great victory he was offered capital to help found the Ford Motor Company. The new company soon became well established. Some of the credit for this came from his breaking of the world speed record in 1903 at 91·378 m.p.h. (147 km.p.h.), but the main reason for his success was that he saw the motor car as a reliable means of transport for the masses. To achieve this he standardised his components wherever possible and cut costs to a minimum.

The Model A Ford was introduced in 1903 and was the first of several successful models produced by the company in the early years. In 1908 the legendary Model T was announced. The Model T was the world's best selling car until the V.W. Beetle came along and, in almost twenty years of production, 15,007,033 vehicles were sold. The Model T was the first car to be produced on a moving assembly line – it was the world's first mass-produced vehicle.

During the whole of the production run, the mechanical components of the Model T were virtually unchanged but various body styles were offered. The model in this book is of the early brass radiator, flat scuttle model of 1913 and is an open 2 seater coupe.

The Model T was affectionately known as the Tin Lizzie and was used for all sorts of unlikely jobs – it even served as a tractor for small farmers. Sales and service depots were established in many countries and the name Ford became known world-wide.

In recent years the Model T Ford has become the most sought after vehicle by the Hot Rod enthusiasts. Fibreglass replica bodies are available because original cars are very hard to find and expensive to buy. Most of these replica Model T's are built on a new chassis and have powerful V8 engines which give them fantastic performance compared with the original 20 h.p. engine and very modest top speed.

'HOT ROD'

MODEL T

FORD

U.S.A.

1913 MODEL T

Length: 3450 mm (136 ins)

Wheelbase: 2540 mm (100 ins)

Engine: 4 cylinders   2·896 cc
developing 20 b.h.p.

Parts required:

1 Balsa base 82 mm × 40 mm × 5 mm
   ($3\frac{1}{4}$ ins × $1\frac{9}{16}$ ins × $\frac{3}{16}$ in)
Windscreen frame 1·5 mm square
   ($\frac{1}{16}$ in) balsa

1 Bulkhead/Floor
1 Body
1 Seat back
1 Seat base
1 Bonnet/Radiator
1 Boot
1 Mudguard
5 Wheels 25 mm diameter × 3 mm
   (1 in × $\frac{1}{8}$ in)

Construction:

1. The balsa base should be prepared as shown. Make the windscreen frame and glue in place.

2. Cut out the bulkhead/floor and body and glue together after doubling over the strengthening pieces which provide a tab for the sloping part of the floor. The tab on the front of the sides is sandwiched between the two parts of the bulkhead.

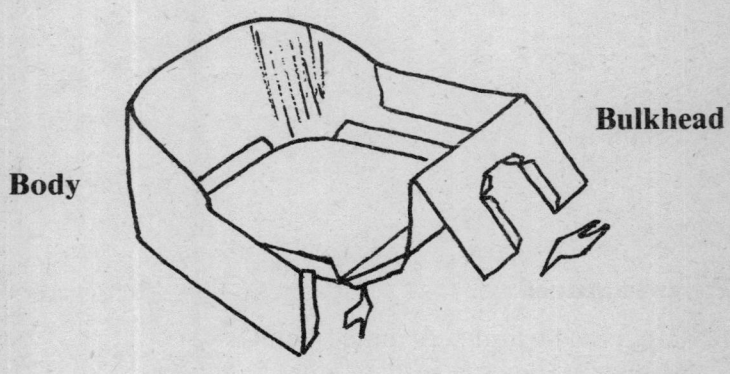

Body

Bulkhead

Assembly of body

The body is now glued to the base and the bonnet prepared and fixed to the base and the tabs on the bulkhead.

The boot is assembled and glued to the base and the back of the body. The seat back and base are fixed in place.

Top view of model showing positions of parts

3. The mudguards are cut out. The centre section is glued under the base and the wings fixed as shown.

   The spare wheel is mounted on the back or on top of the boot.

   The model is finished by adding steering column and wheel (see Mercedes p. 93), lights, etc.

Paint your model the colour of your choice but remember that the Ford catalogue stated that customers could choose any colour they liked 'as long as it was black'!

Plans

Base

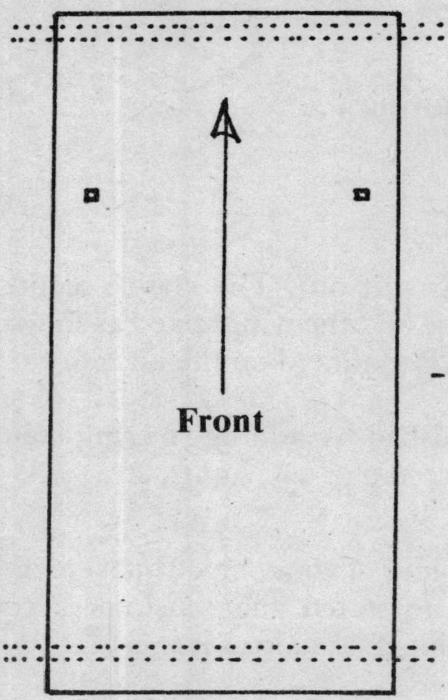

Front

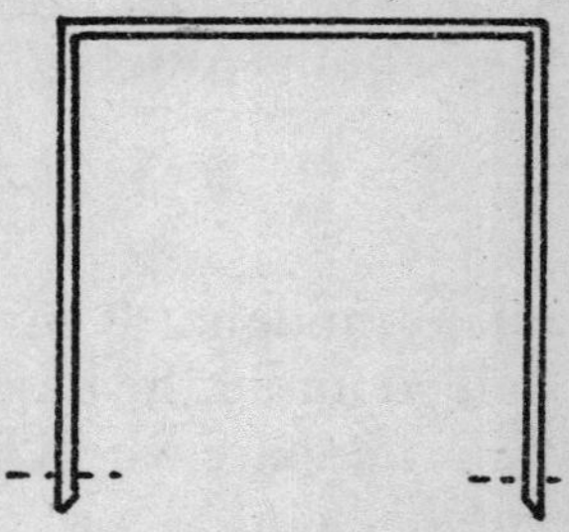

Windscreen

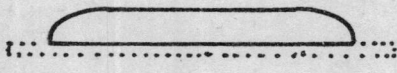

Cross section of base

Body

Seat back

Seat base

Bonnet radiator

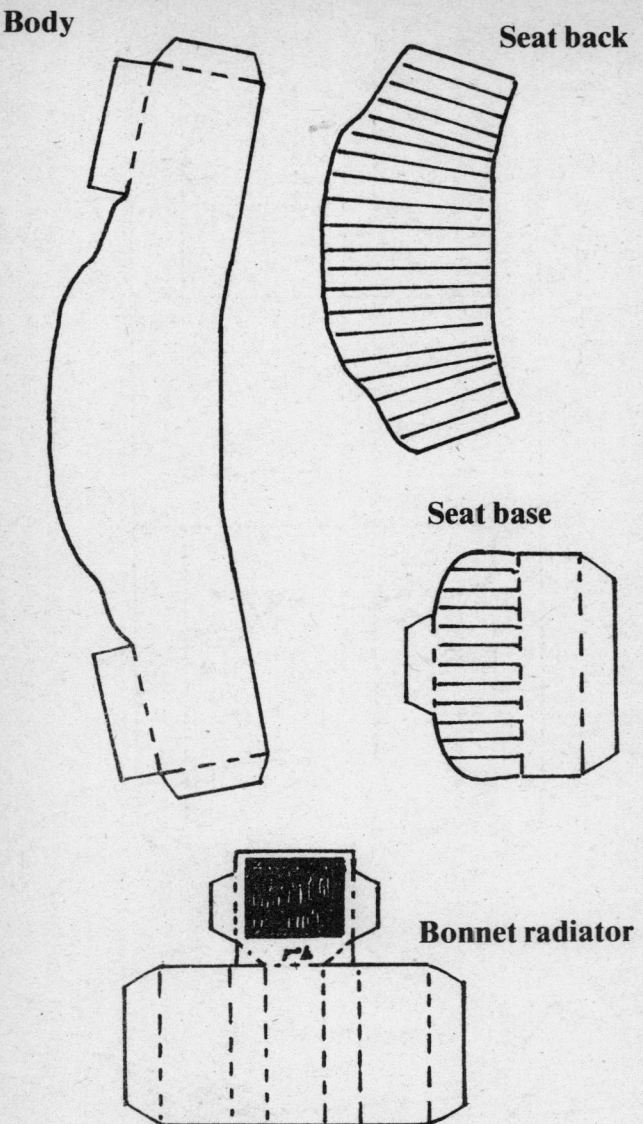

Mudguard

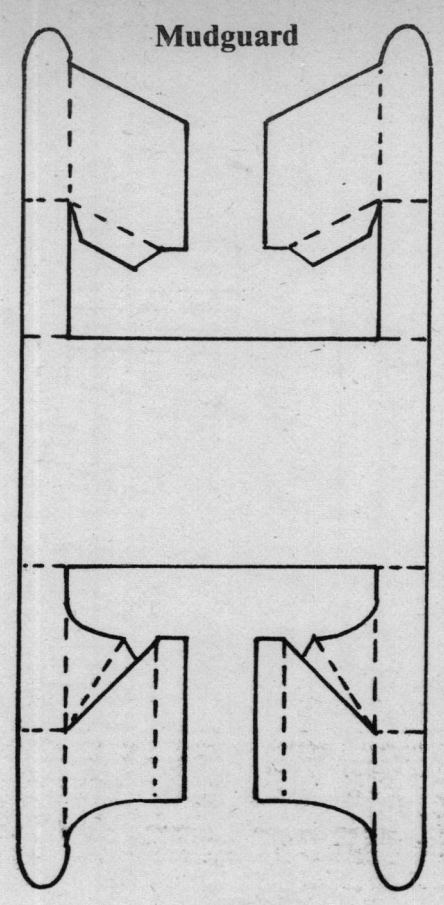

Assembly details

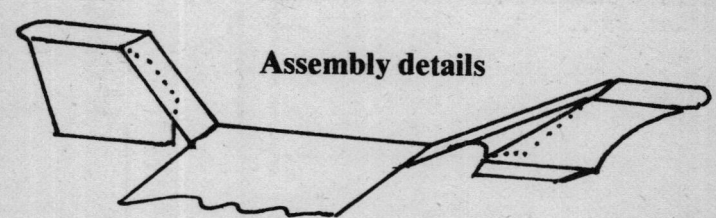

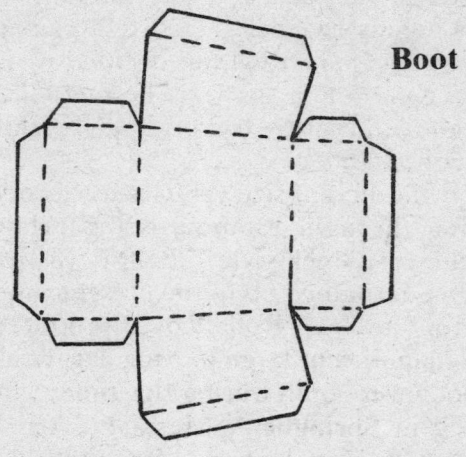

Boot

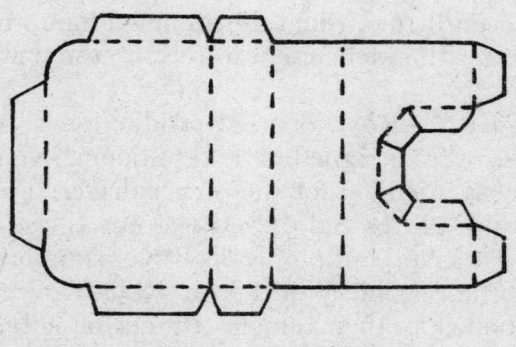

Bulkhead/Floor

ROLLS ROYCE

Henry Royce was a manufacturer of electrical items in Manchester at the turn of the century when he became interested in motor vehicles. He was appalled at the poor quality of the cars he saw and decided in 1903 to build cars to his own design. In 1904 he met Charles Rolls, a motor dealer, and the two set up a partnership to produce and sell high quality cars.

A range of different size vehicles was produced and all were built to the highest standards, regardless of cost. The famous elegant Greek-style radiator was used from the start and has remained up to the present time.

From 1906 to 1925 Rolls Royce produced the 'Silver Ghost', a magnificent large touring car with a seven litre engine. 8000 were built during this time, 1700 of them at the factory in Springfield, Massachusetts, U.S.A., and won for the company the reputation for the 'best car in the world'. It was a very dignified car and invariably looked after by a full-time chauffeur.

The Silver Ghost was replaced by the Phantom 1 in 1925, the new car chassis was similar to the Ghost but the engine was much modified. In 1929 the Phantom II was introduced with a new and much improved chassis which continued until 1935 when the all new Phantom III was introduced with independent front suspension and a V12 engine.

In 1922 Rolls Royce started production of a smaller car, Ghosts were designed to be chauffeur driven and the new car was intended for the owner-driver. The engine was just over 3 litres and the car was not as fast as bigger ones but it was still built to 'Rolls Royce standards'.

Before the Second World War Rolls Royce did not produce bodies for their vehicles, the customer bought the complete chassis and had the coachwork built to suit his own requirements and some of these bodies have been the most elegant and expensive the world has ever seen. In recent years complete cars have been produced with some of the original coach-building firms being taken over by Rolls Royce.

The Rolls Royce still claims the title 'Best car in the world' and is used by Royalty and heads of state in many countries as it has been from the earliest days.

The model that follows is of a Phantom II of the early thirties. The style of bodywork was popular at that time – the roof was fabric covered to give the car the drop-head look and the wide doors gave access to the rear seats. The appearance was very elegant but was also quite sporting and appealed to the wealthy owner-driver.

ROLLS ROYCE PHANTOM II 1934

ROLLS ROYCE ENGLAND

PHANTOM II 1934

Length: 4826 mm (190 ins)

Wheelbase: 3657 mm (144 ins)

Engine: 6 cylinder 7668 cc

(Rolls Royce have never disclosed the power developed by their engines, they claim that it is 'adequate'.)

Parts required:

1 Balsa base 156 mm × 44 mm × 5 mm
($6\frac{1}{8}$ ins × $1\frac{3}{4}$ ins × $\frac{3}{16}$ in)
2 Sides
1 Windscreen bulkhead
1 Body bulkhead
1 Roof/Windscreen
1 Radiator
1 Bonnet
1 Luggage trunk
2 Front wings
2 Rear wing backs
2 Rear wings
5 Wheels 25 mm diameter × 5 mm
(1 in × 0·2 in)
2 Axles 1·5 mm diameter × 55 mm
($\frac{1}{16}$ in × $2\frac{1}{4}$ ins)
Bumpers from 1·5 mm × 5 mm balsa
($\frac{1}{16}$ in × $\frac{3}{16}$ in)

Headlights from scrap balsa or cut from felt-tip pen lids 10 mm ($\frac{3}{8}$ in) diameter.

Construction:

This is perhaps the most complicated model in the book but, if you take care, should not be too difficult.

1. Prepare the balsa base and attach the sides. The front end of the sides is fixed at the position of the front axle. The windscreen bulkhead is glued in place at the angle of the screen pillars and the body bulkhead is fitted at the back of the side windows. The rear of the body is made from the back of the sides rolled round and glued together and to the base.

2. The windscreen/roof can now be fitted, the screen is glued over the bulkhead, and the tabs at its lower edge are bent square for fixing the bonnet.

   The radiator should now be prepared and glued in place, followed by the bonnet.

Bonnet

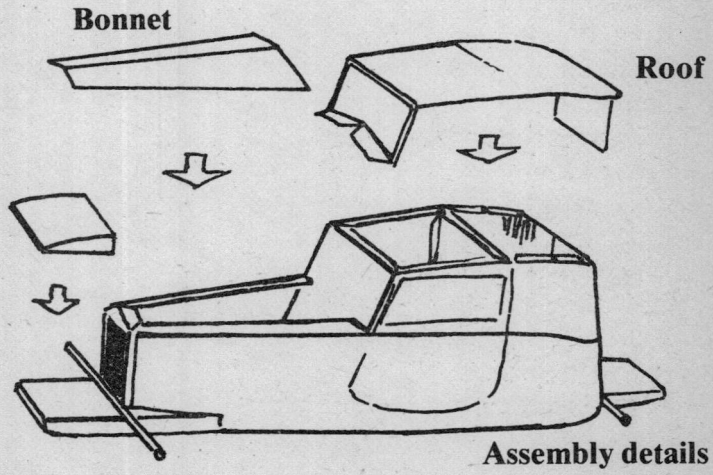

Roof

Assembly details

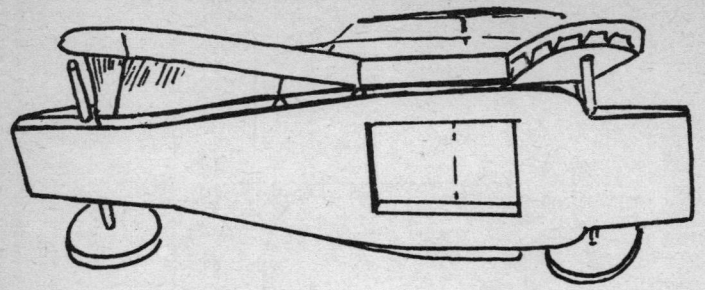

Underside showing fixing of wings

The wings should be prepared and fitted as shown. The luggage trunk should be assembled and glued to the back of the body and to the base.

3. The model is finished by adding a thin dowel or strip of balsa between the front wings to support them and carry the headlights. Fit the bumpers, cutting them to size and glueing one to each end of the chassis. Glue the road wheels to the axles and trim the bottom of the spare wheel, mounting it on the back of the luggage trunk.

Front view

Dotted line shows front bumper

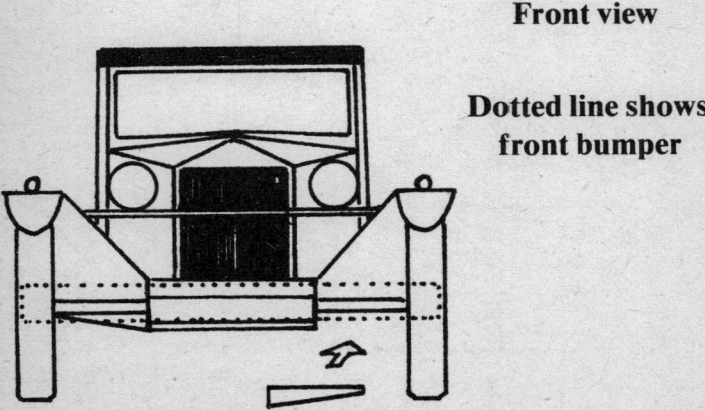

Plans

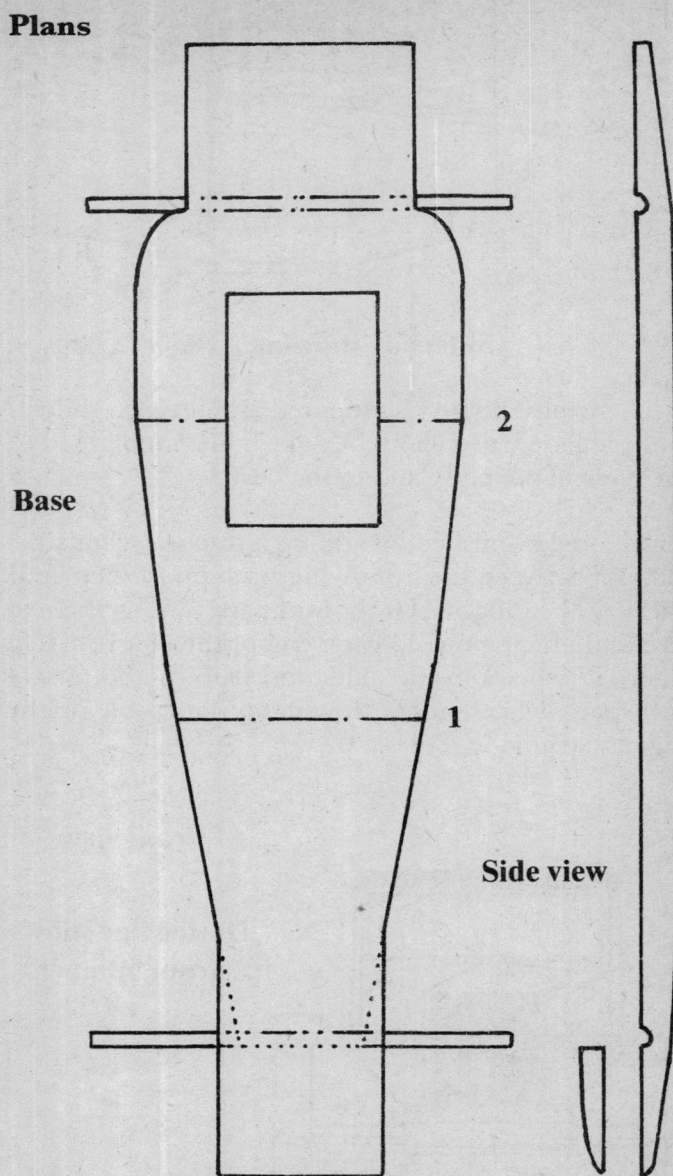

Base

2

1

Side view

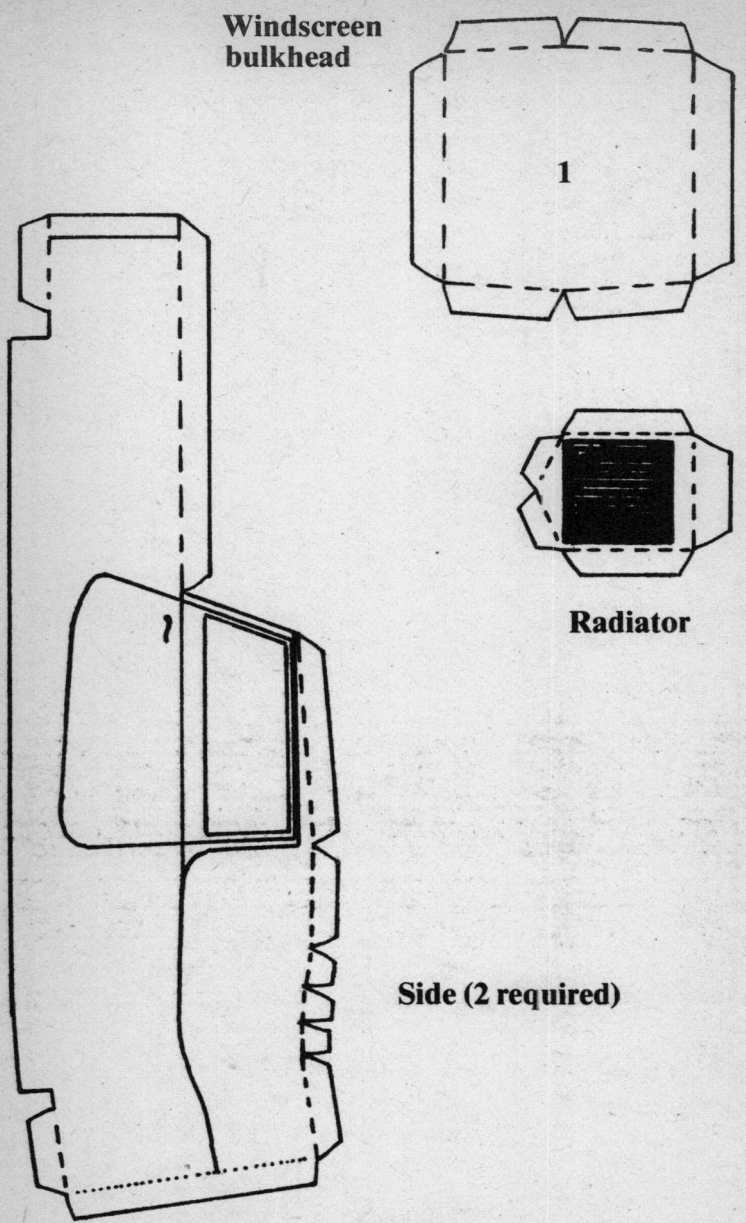

Windscreen bulkhead

1

Radiator

Side (2 required)

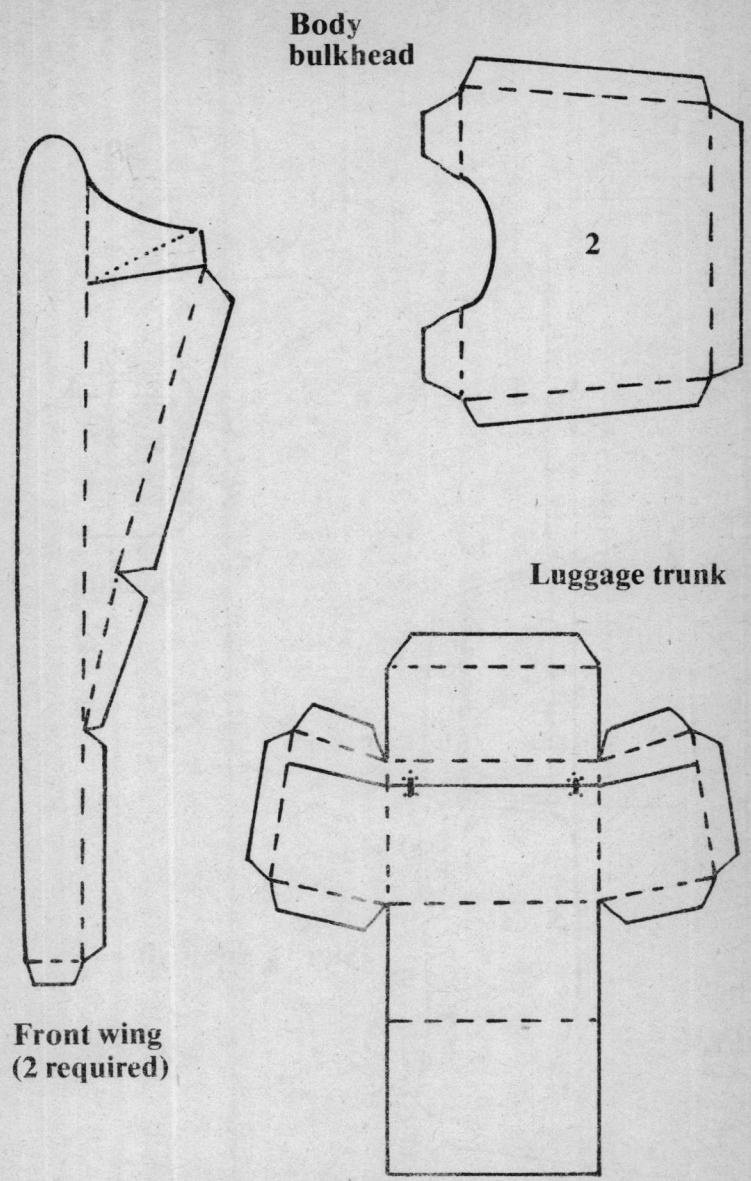

**Body
bulkhead**

2

Luggage trunk

**Front wing
(2 required)**

Roof/Windscreen

**Rear wing
(2 required)**

Bonnet

**Rear wing back
(2 required)**

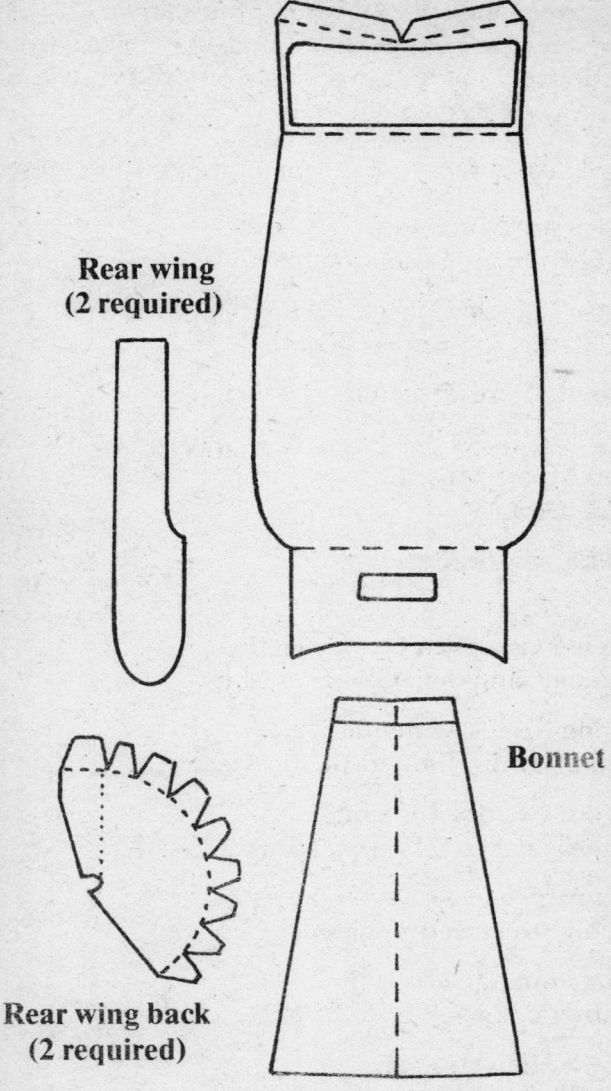

Collections and Museums

There are many places where you can see interesting motor vehicles. Your local museum may have a transport collection and many garages have restored vintage cars in their showrooms.

Below is a list of some of the major motor museums:

The Science Museum,
South Kensington, London S.W.1.

Historic Vehicle Collection of Mr. C. M. Booth,
High Street, Rolvenden, Kent.

National Motor Museum,
Beaulieu, Hants.

Totnes Motor Museum,
Totnes, Devon.

Cheddar Motor Museum,
Somerset.

Chipping Campden Car Collection.
Chipping Campden, Gloucestershire.

Midland Motor Museum,
Stanmore Hall, Bridgnorth, Shropshire.

Stratford Motor Museum,
Stratford on Avon, Warwickshire.

Museum of Science and Industry,
Newhall Street, Birmingham.

The Donnington Collection,
Donnington Park, Castle Donnington, Derby.

Stanford Hall Museum,
Lutterworth, Leicestershire.

Banham International Motor Museum,
Nr. Norwich, Norfolk

Caister Castle Motor Museum,
Caister on Sea, Norfolk.

Autoworld,
South Shore, Blackpool, Lancs.

Hull Transport Museum,
Kingston upon Hull, Humberside.

Man Motor Museum,
Crosby, Isle of Man.

The Transport Museum,
Witham Street, Belfast.

Pembrokeshire Motor Museum,
Pembroke Dock, Dyfed, S. Wales.

Doune Motor Museum,
Doune, Scotland.

Myreton Motor Museum,
Aberlady, Lothian.

Glasgow Museum of Transport,
Albert Drive, Glasgow.

Transport Museum,
Covent Garden, London.

MAKING MODEL AEROPLANES by Peter Fairhurst
0 552 540994
45p
Non-fiction

If you had been alive a hundred years ago, you would probably never . have ridden a bicycle, you would certainly never had a ride in a car, and if someone said that he wanted to fly like a bird, you would have thought he was a dreamer.

All this was soon to change, when in 1903 the Wright brothers made four powered flights. Man could at last fly like the birds.

MAKING MODEL AEROPLANES shows you how to make some of these early planes such as the *Antoinette VII* and the *Bleriot XI* as well as aeroplanes used in the Second World War like the *Spitfire*, and *Messerschmitt*.

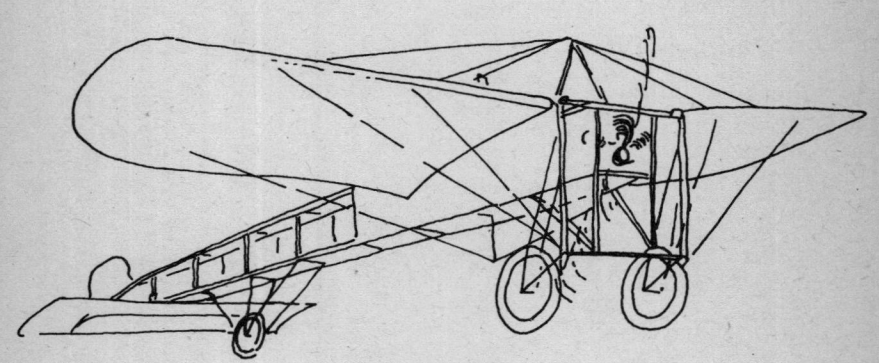

MAKING MODEL TRANSPORT VEHICLES by
Peter Fairhurst   45P
0 552 54122 2   Non-fiction

If you like making models, and you are interested in
trucks and lorries and all transport vehicles, then this is
the book for you.

There are vans, transporters, fire engines, oil tankers,
tippers and articulated lorries, all with detailed plans and
easy to follow instructions.

All these heavy duty vehicles are made to the same scale as
that used in **MAKING MODEL CARS**, so that the
models can be used and displayed together.

If you would like to receive a newsletter telling you
about our new children's books, fill in the coupon
with your name and address and send it to:

Gillian Osband,
Transworld Publishers Ltd,
Century House,
61-63 Uxbridge Road, Ealing,
London, W5 5SA

Name ....

Address ....

....

....

CHILDREN'S NEWSLETTER

All the books on the previous pages are available at your bookshop or can
be ordered direct from Transworld Publishers Ltd., Cash Sales Dept.,
P.O. Box 11, Falmouth, Cornwall.
Please send full name and address together with cheque or postal order
— no currency, and allow 22p per book to cover postage and packing
(plus 10p each for additional copies).